John P. Jenning
3/1/32

CRIMINAL JUSTICE IN AMERICA

COLVER LECTURES

HUMAN LIFE AS THE BIOLOGIST SEES IT
By VERNON KELLOGG

THE RISE OF UNIVERSITIES
By CHARLES H. HASKINS

THE NATURE OF LIFE
By W. J. V. OSTERHOUT

AMERICA AND WORLD PEACE
By HONORABLE JOHN H. CLARKE

TYPES OF SOCIETY IN MEDIEVAL LITERATURE
By FREDERICK TUPPER

MYSTIC ITALY
By M. ROSTOVTZEFF

BACKGROUND OF THE RUSSIAN REVOLUTION
By BARON ALEXANDER MEYENDORFF

WHEN THE WEST IS GONE
By FREDERIC L. PAXSON

CRIMINAL JUSTICE IN AMERICA
By ROSCOE POUND

Published by
HENRY HOLT AND COMPANY

CRIMINAL JUSTICE
IN AMERICA

By

ROSCOE POUND

CARTER PROFESSOR OF JURISPRUDENCE
IN HARVARD UNIVERSITY

NEW YORK

HENRY HOLT AND COMPANY

COPYRIGHT, 1930,
BY
BROWN UNIVERSITY

PRINTED IN THE
UNITED STATES OF AMERICA

To
THEODORE FRANCIS GREEN

PREFACE

These lectures have been written out from the notes used at the time of their delivery (1923). In the years which have intervened much has happened, but little, I think, to change the main lines of the picture or important details. Occasionally a reference to subsequent events has been interpolated; but with these few exceptions the lectures speak from the date of their delivery and represent what I then thought and said. This caution seems expedient lest they should appear to pass a present judgment on what I am now required to look into more deeply.

R. P.

Washington,
November 7, 1929.

CONTENTS

ix

CONTENTS

The Colver lectureship is provided by a fund of $10,000 (it was afterwards increased to $15,000) presented to Brown University by Mr. and Mrs. Jesse L. Rosenberger of Chicago in memory of Mrs. Rosenberger's father, Charles K. Colver of the class of 1842. The following sentences from the letter accompanying the gift explain the purposes of the foundation:—

"It is desired that, so far as possible, for these lectures only subjects of particular importance and lecturers eminent in scholarship or of other marked qualifications shall be chosen. It is desired that the lectures shall be distinctive and valuable contributions to human knowledge, known for their quality rather than their number. Income, or portions of income, not used for lectures may be used for the publication of any of the lectures deemed desirable to be so published."

Charles Kendrick Colver (1821-1896) was a graduate of Brown University of the class of 1842. The necrologist of the University wrote of him: "He was distinguished for his broad and accurate scholarship, his unswerving personal integrity, championship of truth, and obedience to God in his daily life. He was severely simple and unworldly in character."

1916

The American Conception of Liberty and Government, by FRANK JOHNSON GOODNOW, LL.D., President of Johns Hopkins University.

1917

Medical Research and Human Welfare, by W. W. KEEN, M.D., LL.D. (Brown), Emeritus Professor of Surgery, Jefferson Medical College, Philadelphia.

1918

The Responsible State; A Reëxamination of Fundamental Political Doctrines in the Light of World

War and the Menace of Anarchism, by FRANKLIN HENRY GIDDINGS, LL.D., Professor of Sociology and the History of Civilization in Columbia University; sometime Professor of Political Science in Bryn Mawr College.

1919

Democracy: Discipline. Peace, by WILLIAM ROSCOE THAYER.

1920

Plymouth and the Pilgrims, by ARTHUR LORD.

1921

Human Life as the Biologist Sees It, by VERNON KELLOGG, Sc.D., LL.D., Secretary National Research Council; sometime Professor in Stanford University.

1922

The Nature of Life, by W. J. V. OSTERHOUT, Professor of Botany, Harvard University.

1923

The Rise of Universities, by CHARLES H. HASKINS, Ph.D., LL.D., Litt.D., Gurney Professor of History and Political Science, in Harvard University.

1924

Criminal Justice in America, by ROSCOE POUND, Ph.D., LL.M., LL.D., D.C.L., Carter Professor of General Jurisprudence and Dean of the Faculty of Law in Harvard University.

1925

America and World Peace, by HONORABLE JOHN H. CLARKE, former Justice of the Supreme Court of the United States.

1926

Types of Society in Medieval Literature, by FREDERICK TUPPER, Ph.D., L.H.D., Professor of the English Language and Literature, University of Vermont.

1927

Mystic Italy, by M. ROSTOVTZEFF, Professor of Ancient History, Yale University.

1928

Background of the Russian Revolution, by BARON ALEXANDER MEYENDORFF, Reader in Russian Laws, Institutions, and Economics in the University of London (sometime member of the Russian State Duma, Senator under the Provisional Government, member of the Constituent Assembly).

1929

When the West Is Gone, by FREDERIC L. PAXSON, Professor of History in the University of Wisconsin.

1930

The History of Science and The New Humanism, by GEORGE SARTON, Associate of the Carnegie Institution of Washington and Editor of *Isis.*

I

THE PROBLEM OF CRIMINAL JUSTICE

The Place of Criminal Justice in Social Control

One way of approaching such problems proceeds in terms of what I have ventured to call social engineering. It conceives of the legal ordering of society as a practical process of eliminating friction and waste in the attainment of human desires. If one likes, he may say that this process is required in order to maintain and further civilization. But the immediate task of social control, of which law is only one item, is a task of adjusting or harmonizing conflicting or overlapping human desires and human claims founded thereon.

From such a standpoint, the end of law is the adjustment or harmonizing of conflicting or overlapping desires and claims, so as to give effect to as much as possible with the least sacrifice. It is the same as the end of all social control. The legal order is but that part of social control which is achieved through the activity of politically ordered society. Law is the body of precepts, of rules and traditions of art for applying those precepts, and of received ideals for shaping, supplementing, and developing them, by which this part of social control is carried on. The basis of the authority of law is immediately the power of organized society. But behind that power is the pressure of the desires and claims involved in life in civilized society, which must be satisfied as far as may be, if civilized society is to maintain itself. Ultimately the law rests upon the basis of its accord with the conditions of life in civilized society.

Hence, today jurists approach the law from psychology rather than from metaphysics. They think of the scope and subject matter of law from the standpoint of the concrete desires and claims of individual men in civilized society, not from the standpoint of the abstract qualities of the abstract individual, nor from the standpoint of the logical implications of the abstract individual free will. They consider the desires or claims found to be involved respectively in the individual life, in the existence and functioning of the political organization of the given society, and in the general social life therein. They think of the precepts, worked out by experience, discovered by a judicial process of trial and error, found by juristic research, or devised by legislative inventive wisdom, whereby these desires are adjusted and given effect, or the resulting claims are secured, so far as may be, in a systematic, ordered social control through politically organized society.

Law does but a part of this whole task of social control; and the criminal law does but a part of that portion which belongs to the law. The household, through its internal discipline and through the pressure of the opinion of its members brought to bear on

particular members, has always been an agency of
the first importance. Also religious organizations,
fraternal organizations, social clubs, professional and
trade organizations, and the like, operate through
their internal discipline to order the conduct of their
members and to restrain them from anti-social activities. In the past, these organizations, whereby the
force of the opinion of one's fellow members may be
brought to bear upon him, have played no small part
in maintaining civilized society. At present, there
are signs of renewed and increasing efficacy of such
agencies of social control. But for centuries such
organizations have operated more and more in sub-
ordination to and by way of supplement to the law.
The state has achieved almost a complete monopoly
of force as a regulative instrument. A minimum of
self-help is grudgingly recognized for certain exceptional situations. Even organized bringing to bear
of general opinion upon particular individuals (e.g.,
in boycotts) is scrutinized jealously by the law and
may result in liability to make reparation, or may be
stopped by injunction, unless directed to the protection of what the law recognizes as a legitimate interest of those who take part therein.

If we take, as it were, an inventory of the concrete
claims which press upon the law for satisfaction and
seek to classify those which the law recognizes and
endeavors to secure, they fall conveniently into
three groups: Individual interests, public interests,
and social interests. By individual interests we mean
claims or demands of individual human beings when

regarded immediately as such. The law, which operates through general precepts, generalizes interests before recognizing and securing them. Individual interests are claims or demands generalized in terms of the individual life. Public interests are the claims, asserted, it is true, by individuals, which are made in the name of or on behalf of a politically organized society. They are demands generalized in terms of political life. It is convenient to treat them as the claims of a politically organized society thought of as a legal entity. Social interests are claims or demands of individual human beings when thought of in terms of social life and generalized as claims of the social group. They are the claims which are involved in the maintenance, the activity and the functioning of society, generalized from that standpoint. It is convenient to treat them as the claims of the whole social group as such. Summarily stated, these social interests may be said to be: The general security, the security of social institutions, the general morals, the conservation of social resources, the general progress, and the individual life.

In any scheme of social interests, first place must be given to the claim or demand, asserted in the name of the social group and generalized in terms of social life, to be secured against those forms of action or courses of conduct which threaten the social existence. This paramount claim may be called the social interest in the general security. It has many forms. In its simplest form it is an interest in the general safety, long recognized legally in the maxim that the safety of the people is the highest law. In another form, well recognized since the nature and causes of epidemic disease have come to be understood, it is an interest in the general health. In another form it is an interest in peace and public order. In an economically developed society, it takes on two other closely related forms, namely, an interest in the security of acquisitions and an interest in the security of transactions.

We maintain the general security by means of social institutions. Hence we may put second an interest in the security of social institutions; the claim or demand involved in life in civilized society that its fundamental institutions be secure from those forms of action and courses of conduct which threaten their existence or impair their efficient functioning. This interest has four forms. It is an interest in the security of domestic institutions, of religious institutions, of political institutions, and of economic institutions. In the earlier history of the law, the first and second were most stressed. In the law of today the stress is rather upon the first and third. Recently the fourth has pressed for recognition.

Third, we may put the claim or demand, involved in life in civilized society, to be secured against acts or courses of conduct subversive of good morals or offensive to the moral sense of the general body of individuals. This may be called the social interest in the general morals. It is an interest in the security of the received ethical custom of the community as a social institution.   At common law infringements of this interest are misdemeanors.

Another important social interest is the claim or demand, involved in life in civilized society, that the goods of existence shall not be wasted.   Where all human claims or demands may not be satisfied, in view of infinite individual desires and limited natural means of satisfying them, there is a claim that acts or courses of conduct which tend needlessly to impair these goods shall be restrained.   This may be called the social interest in the conservation of social resources.

By the social interest in general progress we mean the claim or demand, involved in social life, that the development of human powers and of human control over nature, for the satisfaction of human wants, go forward.   It is a demand that what I have called social engineering be increasingly and continually improved.   As it were, it is the self-assertion of the group toward higher and more complete development of human powers.   On its negative side, it calls upon us to restrain all interference with agencies of economic, political, or cultural progress.

Lastly, there is the social interest in the individual life.   One might call it the social interest in the individual moral and social life, or in the individual human life.   It is the claim or demand that, if all individual desires may not be satisfied, they be satisfied at least so far as is reasonably possible and to the extent of a minimum human life.   Three forms of this interest have been recognized in common law or in legislation. One might be called the social interest in individual free self-assertion, physical, mental, and economic. Another might be called the social interest in individual opportunity; the claim or demand, involved in social life, that all individuals shall have fair opportunities, political, physical, social, and economic. In a third form, the social interest in the individual life appears as a claim that each individual shall have secured to him the conditions of at least a minimum human life under the circumstances of life in the time and place.

Such, in outline, are the social interests which are recognized or are coming to be recognized in modern law. Not only do these claims often shade into one another, but often they overlap or conflict. Not infrequently a particular individual claim may be referred to more than one of the foregoing social interests according to the connection in which it is asserted or the standpoint from which it is regarded in weighing it against other claims. Looked at functionally, the legal ordering of society is an attempt to satisfy or harmonize or adjust these overlapping and often conflicting claims and demands, either through securing them directly and immediately, or through securing certain individual interests, or delimitations or compromises of individual interests, so as to give effect to the most that is possible of the whole scheme of social interests, or to the interests which weigh most in our civilization, with the least sacrifice of the scheme of interests as a whole. In

order to do this, the law selects the claims which it
recognizes and seeks to secure, delimits them with
reference to other interests, and sets up an apparatus
of rights, duties, liabilities, powers, and privileges, by
which to secure them, and an enforcing machinery by
which to make this apparatus effective in action.
Thus, with respect to any interest, the law has to determine its *de facto* extent, to put a value upon it in
comparison with competing interests, to ascertain
how far it may be given effect by means of legal machinery, and to devise the appropriate machinery for
giving it effect.

It is the province of criminal law to secure social
interests regarded directly as such, that is, disso-
ciated from any immediate individual interests with
which they might be identified. The chief reliance of
modern legal systems for the immediate securing of
such interests is the imposition of what Austin called
absolute duties. The law imposes duties of doing
certain things or of abstaining from certain acts or
courses of conduct without conferring any corresponding or correlative individual legal right. It
provides for the enforcement of such duties by criminal prosecution, and the imposition of some sort of
penal treatment in case of conviction. In consequence, over and above the general problems involved
in all securing of interests by means of the law, criminal law has special problems. It must define absolute
duties so as to preserve a just and workable balance
between the competing social interests involved. It
must safeguard the general security and the indi-

vidual life against abuse of criminal procedure, while
at the same time making that procedure as effective
as possible for the securing of the whole scheme of
social interests.   It must devise effective enforcing
agencies, both punitive and preventive, while at the
same time giving due effect to the interest in the individual life.

Complaints of Want of Respect for and Non-En-
forcement of Law, and Their Relation to the
Conditions of Criminal Justice Today.

At the end of the eighteenth century and in the
nineteenth century men were most concerned about
the individual life.   They stressed the limitations
upon interference with individual liberty and the
checks imposed to prevent arbitrary magisterial action.   Just now men are most concerned about the
general security and efficiency of the enforcing machinery.   Indeed, the present century has seen an
increase of interest in criminal law throughout the
world.   In Great Britain, two series of notable criminal trials have been publishing, and there is a constantly increasing literature on crime and criminals.
In the United States, the Institute of Criminal Law
and Criminology, surveys of criminal justice in many
localities, the National Commission on Law Observance and Enforcement, the National Crime Commission, and many like state and local commissions, continually increasing attention to criminal law on the
part of the American Bar Association, as well as a

steadily growing literature on crime, criminals, and criminal justice—all these things tell the same story. For the Continent, we may vouch projects for revision of penal codes or for new codes, study of comparative criminal law, and a like increase in the literature of criminal law and related subjects. Quite apart from special reasons which, especially since the war, have focussed attention on criminal law and its enforcement in the United States, there have been conditions of world-wide operation making everywhere for greater attention to this part of the legal ordering of society.

With us, along with new and growing interest in every phase of criminal justice go complaints of want of respect for law and that the precepts of the criminal law are not enforced. There is nothing new in this. Complaint of non-enforcement is as old as the law itself. It has been loud in this country from the beginning. The most one may allow is that impatience of legal restraint and complaint that laws are not enforced are more acute at some times than at others. Nor is it hard to see why both should be well marked in America at this time. Within a generation there have been profound changes in the background of social control to which all its agencies must be adjusted. The points at which the claims and desires of each individual and those of his fellows conflict or overlap have increased enormously. Likewise new agencies of menace to the general security have developed in profusion. In consequence, the volume of legal precepts regulating individual conduct and

governing individual relations has increased beyond
experience. The economic unification of the country
has gone forward so rapidly and so completely that
our administrative machinery has become inadequate
and all kinds of new administrative agencies have
been springing up, with jurisdictional lines, methods,
and modes of review still to be worked out. If there
were nothing else to be considered, these things would
suffice to make it difficult for the individual citizen
to know the details of the mass of penally sanctioned
rules by which his conduct is governed, or to appreciate the reasons which lie behind them. Many necessary restrictions on offhand individual action, when
first brought to his notice, seem arbitrary or even
needless. Moreover, the machinery of enforcement,
by which we seek to give effect to the huge mass of
penally sanctioned rules, was devised for a simpler
society, in which the number of precepts to be enforced was much less, in which the precepts themselves were simpler and had to do with simpler situations, and in which the facts involved in the general
run of prosecutions were of a sort to be understood
readily by magistrates and by jurors.

In our nineteenth-century polity the home was a
chief reliance. The household was a unit, social, economic, and legal. Domestic discipline was legally
recognized and was a reality. Such things as one of
the household haling another into court were tolerated only in extreme cases, and were repugnant to
the settled policy of the law. Likewise neighborhood
opinion was effective. Although the neighborhood

had ceased to be a legal unit since the Middle Ages, it was a social and economic unit, and the pressure exerted upon the individual neighbor was strong. Above all, organized religion included the great majority of men in well knit groups. Religious training was all but universal, and the pressure of the church group and its opinion of things which were done and things which were not done was exerted upon every one. Obviously the hold of all these is much less in the urban, industrial society of today. The household is no longer an economic unit and there are little more than vestiges of its legal unity. There is a radical change in the policy of the law as to legal proceedings by children against parents, and domestic discipline is relaxed to the point of extinction. The neighborhood is no longer an economic unit. Large numbers of persons are carried in and out of business centers every day, to live their economic lives in one place, with one set of associates, and their social lives elsewhere with different associates. One's everyday relationships are not necessarily with his neighbors. A dweller in an apartment house is as likely not to know them as the dweller in the rural community of our formative era was unable to escape knowing them. Thus we must rely on the law and the policeman for much which was once in the province of neighborhood opinion. As to organized religion, its lessened hold is manifest.

This complete change in the background of social control involves much that may easily be attributed to ineffectiveness of criminal justice, and yet means only that it is called on to do the whole work, where once it shared its task with other agencies and was invoked, not for every occasion, but exceptionally.

From this change in the background of criminal justice and from the multiplication of points of contact between man and man, and increased conflict of interests, incident to urban life and an industrial society, there results a corresponding multiplication of laws. Rhode Island is by no means an extreme case. Relatively, penal legislation in Rhode Island is not voluminous. In California the Penal Code contains 1616 sections, covering the same ground as Titles XXXIX, XL, and XLI of the General Statutes of Rhode Island of 1923, which contain in all 657 sections. In Illinois, the current edition of the statutes requires four volumes, each about as large as the single volume of the General Laws of Rhode Island for 1923. In Missouri the current edition of the statutes is in six volumes, in Ohio in seven volumes, in New York in eight volumes. In Missouri the total number of sections in the statute law of the state is (or at least was recently) 13,672. In Michigan it is, or was recently, 15,532. In Ohio it was recently 15,367. In the General Laws of Rhode Island for 1923, the whole number of sections is 6,768. To take Rhode Island for an example, then, is very conservative. Taking this state for our example of what has been going on throughout the land, a comparison of penal legislation as it was one hundred years ago, as it was fifty years ago, and as it is today, will reveal much.

In the Revised Public Laws of Rhode Island of 1822, the "Act to Reform the Penal Laws" defines fifty crimes. In the General Statutes of 1872, Title XXX, "Of Crimes and Punishments," defines one hundred and twenty-eight crimes. In the General Laws of 1923, in Title XXXIX, "Of Crimes and Punishment," the number has grown to two hundred and twelve. Thus there are now more than four times as many punishable offenses prescribed by the title on crimes as there were one hundred years ago, and there has been an increase of sixty per cent. in this title in fifty years. But this is far from the whole story. Today the Title "Of Crimes and Punishment" does not contain half of the offenses that may be prosecuted by the state and may be visited with fine or imprisonment, or both. One important new title in the General Laws of 1923, as compared with the General Statutes of 1872, is Title X, "Of Labor and Industry." The following chapters in that title, each involving more than one penally sanctioned offense, to be prosecuted by the state, are significant of relatively new conditions in American criminal justice: Chapter 85, "Of Factory Inspection," Chapter 89, "Of Sanitary Accommodations in Factories," Chapter 92, "Of Payments to Employees for Personal Injuries Received in the Course of their Employment, and of the Prevention of Such Injuries," Chapter 93, "Of the Protection of Employees during the Erection of Buildings," Chapter 94, "Of the Inspection of and Fixing a Standard for the Construction of Boilers."

Again, in 1872 there were twenty chapters in Title XIV, "Of Internal Police."   In 1923 that title has expanded into three: XV, "Of Internal Police," XVI, "Of the Public Health," and XVII, "Of Protection from Fire."   The old title "Of Internal Police" now has thirty-four chapters, and the new titles have eighteen chapters and seven chapters respectively.   Thus in this connection alone there are fifty-nine chapters where fifty years ago there were but twenty, and these new chapters provide fifty-four new offenses non-existent in 1872.   Other significant new chapters in 1923, as compared with 1872, are: Chapter 98, "Of Motor Vehicles and the Operation Thereof," Chapter 127, "Of Enforcing the Prohibition of Intoxicating Liquors for Beverage Purposes," Chapter 273, "Of the Regulation of the Sale of Securities," Chapter 311, "Of Sales of Merchandise in Bulk," Chapter 315, "Of Criminal Offenses Relative to Warehouse Receipts," and Chapter 320, "Of Criminal Offenses Relative to Bills of Lading." This catalogue of chapters defining new crimes is very far from exhaustive.   It is enough to say that when all are taken into account, the number of crimes for which one may be prosecuted in Rhode Island has very much more than doubled in fifty years, and has multiplied by eight in one hundred years.

It is no less important to note that multiplication of agencies of menace to the general security has quite outrun our experience of coping with them, and often has somewhat rapidly outrun the ability of the average citizen to appreciate their relation to the life of the community of today. Within one hundred years the advent of the railroad made over—one might almost say made—our modern law of civil injuries. When the law had been reasonably adjusted to the conditions involved in railroad transportation, the precepts devised with reference thereto had to be applied to electric transportation and trolley roads. Then, within less than a generation, came motor vehicles. The coming of the automobile has begun to make new chapters both in the civil and in the criminal law, and is making over other chapters. Indeed, the general use of motor vehicles is affecting the conditions that make for crime, the difficulties of preventing and detecting crime, and the administration of punitive justice.

To the new tasks thrown upon criminal law by the invention and development of the motor vehicle we must add those imposed by new varieties of habit-forming drugs and increased use of such drugs under conditions of crowded urban life. We must take account of industrial disputes under the changed conditions of labor in the American city of today. We must reckon with the conditions of juvenile delinquency in our large cities, which have added a new kind of court to American judicial organization, and new administrative agencies to our apparatus of penal treatment. We must note the changed conditions of life which have called for another novel tribunal in the courts of domestic relations, now set up in more than one city. We must bear in mind new forms of amusement, such

as moving picture theatres, with more than one possibility of menace to the general morals and indirectly
to the general security, and even, as in the case of
combustible films, with new possibilities of danger to
life. We must consider new occupations, dangerous
to those employed therein, and especially to those
employed in large numbers; unhealthy conditions of
work where large numbers are brought together daily
in one plant; increased danger of loss of life through
fires in crowded buildings, whether used for amusements, for industry, or for dwellings; new conditions
of menace in the practice of professions in crowded
urban communities in which there are masses of
ignorant and credulous to be preyed upon; and the
impossibility of insuring wholesome food or pure
drugs and the dangers involved in adulteration, if,
as things are today, the sole resource of the law were
to be civil liability of vendors for resulting injuries
to purchasers. In all these cases, and in many more,
under the conditions of the time, there is serious
menace to the general security in ways which the
ordinary citizen, under the ordinary circumstances of
his experience, does not perceive readily, and is not
likely to appreciate until a gross instance or a whole-
sale disaster shocks the conscience of the community
into a spasm of activity. In the normal condition of
lethargy as to these misdemeanors, where the reasons
grow out of unfamiliar situations, or relatively new
facts of social life, there is little to move the administrative officer, or the individual citizen as a potential complainant, or the public prosecutor, to under-

take the thankless task of proceeding against an individual instance of violation of the law. This is the more true when that instance must be selected from a multitude of other violations of like precepts, which press equally upon his attention or must be undertaken at the expense of other duties of at least equal moment.

Another complicating factor in the administration of criminal justice in present-day America is the rapid and unprecedented growth of urban population in the last generation. The population of New York City multiplied by forty-six in one hundred years. It has multiplied by six in fifty years and almost by four in twenty years. Not much more than a big town in 1820, and not yet with a population of a million in 1870, New York had a population of a million and a half in 1890, of nearly three millions and a half in 1900, and of over five millions and a half in 1920. Again, Chicago was non-existent in 1820, and its population (two million seven hundred thousand in 1920) multiplied by nine in fifty years. Cleveland, which was a village of less than one thousand inhabitants in 1820, had in 1920 a population of nearly eight hundred thousand, and had multiplied its population by more than eight in fifty years. In 1920 Detroit had multiplied its population by thirteen in fifty years, by five in thirty years, and by four in twenty years, and had over a million inhabitants. Los Angeles had multiplied by one hundred in fifty years, by almost twelve in thirty years, and by almost six in twenty years, and had over five hundred and seventy-eight thousand inhabitants where there had been but an Indian mission a hundred years before. In the decade from 1880 to 1890, the growth of population in the United States began to concentrate in large cities. For the past fifty years the growth of the United States from a population of thirty-eight millions to one of one hundred and twenty millions has more and more taken place in a group of large cities—conspicuously in some nineteen cities which in 1880 had each a population of over two hundred thousand, and in a few which have sprung into large size since that date. By 1920, more than half of the population of the United States was to be found in cities.

Prior to 1880, and largely prior to 1890, the great increase in population in this country had been due to progressive settlement and development of new areas in which the rural, agricultural, pioneer conditions of the beginnings of our polity were repeated. This development came to an end a generation ago and was succeeded by a new era of development of densely populated urban areas. It is in such an era that the legal institutions of rural, agricultural, pioneer America must function today, and it is no accident that the definite transition is marked by widespread dissatisfaction with the administration of criminal law.

Diversification of population has gone along with the rapid growth of large cities. In 1900 one third of the population of Chicago were foreign born, and a million, out of a population of about one million seven hundred thousand, spoke languages other than English. In 1920, Chicago had a negro population of one hundred and nine thousand. In 1920, seventy per cent. of the people of Detroit were of foreign birth and represented thirty-four nationalities. In New York City, in 1920, one million nine hundred and eighty-nine thousand, out of a total of five million six hundred and twenty thousand inhabitants, were foreign born, and one hundred and fifty-three thousand were negroes. In other words, the homogeneous rural communities, presupposed by the legal institutions devised in the latter part of the eighteenth century and the first decades of the nineteenth century, had ceased to be the dominant type. A wholly new type of community had arisen, of which our legal institutions had had no experience. In these communities the character and environment of crime are new and the demands upon enforcing agencies, upon police, upon adjudication, and upon penal treatment are quite out of the experience of those who laid out the lines of our legal development and gave shape to our criminal law and procedure.

In three respects especially the change from a rural, agricultural, to an urban, industrial society has affected our criminal justice fundamentally. For one thing, multiplication of legal precepts, required by the crowded conditions of urban life and the development of new agencies of menace to the general security, bears directly upon our chief reliance for the effectiveness of the law in action. Rules of law do not enforce themselves. They obtain in action, as distinguished from their theoretical force in the books, because their social-psychological efficiency is guaranteed; because the authority which has prescribed them is so backed by social-psychological power as to be in a position to give them effect, as motives for action, in spite of countervailing individual motives. Both traditional legal precepts and statutory rules continually fall short of what they are called upon to do, and their falling short is usually largely due to lack of social-psychological guarantee. One rule may run counter to the individual interests of a majority or of a dominant class. Another may run counter to the moral ideas of individuals or of an obstinate minority. In case of another, no immediate desires or claims of individuals may be involved, and the mass of the community may be indifferent. The social legislation demanded by the conditions of the American city or industrial community of today is likely to encounter any or even all of these difficulties. When it is remembered that out of one hundred thousand persons arrested in Chicago in 1912, more than one half were held for violation of legal precepts which did not exist twenty-five years before, with respect to which, therefore, the community had not been educated to a thorough-going appreciation of their importance, it will be seen how much the growth of large cities has contributed to the difficulties of criminal justice on the side of enforcement.

Again, the change to an urban, industrial society, the economic unification of the country and the multiplication of legal precepts, have increased the demand for administrative agencies of enforcement. But, for historical reasons, administration has been the weakest point in our traditional Anglo-American polity. England had strong central government at an earlier date than the rest of the modern world. Also England had strong central courts of general jurisdiction before her neighbors. Hence, before there was much call for administration of a modern type, need had been felt of putting checks upon the English crown in the interest of the individual and of the local community, and strong courts were at hand to impose them. The tendency thus acquired by the common law was intensified during the seventeenth-century contests between courts and crown, and still further intensified by the conditions of the formative period of American law. A pioneer or sparsely settled rural community is content with the necessary minimum of government. Moreover, this pioneer jealousy of governmental action was reinforced by the Puritan's aversion to administrative interference with the individual will. Accordingly, for a time we tied down administration too rigidly. We sought to enforce factory laws, pure food laws, health laws, housing laws, and much more of the sort by prosecutions after the event. We sought to compel administrative officers to deal with cases under these laws as a court would try a prosecution for an old-time offense against person or property. Also we sought to reduce the judicial administration of justice to chapter and verse of written rule on its purely

administrative side. Thus our judicial justice has
been embarrassed for a time by the attempt to do
what is not judicial, and often has fallen short of
what it should be in purely judicial matters. But in
purely administrative phases of criminal justice, our
uncentralized and non-coöperative régime of independent local jurisdictions and of independent authorities working each in its own way in the same
locality is an anachronism in the economically unified land of today.

Moreover, the law has had to do not a little experi-
menting with the new situations with which it has
had to wrestle in the large cities and diversified pop-
ulations of today. In law, as everywhere else, we
have to learn by a process of trial and error. But
in law we tie down experiment by constitutional
guarantees, by a complex machinery of legislative
lawmaking, and by holding courts to the employment
of a traditional technique upon received legal materials. Nevertheless a certain amount of experi-
menting, in order to find the best solution for new
problems, is inevitable; and new problems have
crowded upon us thick and fast in the American city
of the present. Much legislation has had to be experimental. The result has been to make us suspicious of needed legislation and to weaken the hold of
law upon the popular imagination just at the time
when it was most tried and most in need of strong
support. Our old agencies of criminal justice have
been under strain, and our new machinery has been
in large degree experimental. Until experience has

shown us the paths which we may follow with assurance, we must expect ineffectiveness and dissatisfaction.

The Agency of Criminal Justice—Penal Treatment

In a developed legal system sanction is added to legal precepts by punishment, by interference to prevent disobedience, and by reinstatement of things to the position in which they were before disobedience, either specifically or by substitution of some equivalent.   Etymologically, sanction is that which makes a rule of law holy.   The term goes back to the beginnings of Roman law and refers originally to the clause which put a human enactment on the same basis as the divine rules, breach of which involved devotion of the offender to the infernal gods.   In other words, consciously made human laws were fortified by giving them the same consequences as those involved in traditional laws regarded as proceeding from the gods.   It should be noted that punishments are only one class of sanctions, and that motive is not sanction, although a purpose of sanction may be to furnish a motive for obedience.   In primitive law sanction is but feebly developed.   Sanctions, in the sense of enforcing machinery, are institutions of developed law.   As social organization becomes more complex, the tendency is continually toward more effective enforcement of rules of action by the force of politically organized society.

Punishment, imposed by way of vengeance, is the

earliest mode of securing interests or vindicating
rights. Regularly the law begins by using penalties.
Later it learns more effective and discriminating
means of enforcing its precepts. Thus when Roman
law first sought to prevent excessive legacies, which
defeated the claims of those upon whom it was conceived the property of a testator ought to devolve,
legislation imposed a penalty of fourfold upon a
legatee who took more than a stated amount. Later
the simpler course was taken of making void excessive gifts by way of legacy. Again, in the beginning
the law dealt with wrongs of all kinds by imposing
a penalty upon the wrongdoer. Later an idea of
what might be called a penalty of reparation developed. Ultimately, the law attained the idea of reparation as appropriate to civil injuries, leaving punishment to be the engine of the criminal law. Today
punishment is appropriated almost exclusively to enforcement of absolute duties. But there are still remnants here and there of the older condition in which
penalties were relied upon for the enforcement of
private rights. Moreover, when any new subject of
legal action arises, calling for legislation, the tendency is in the first instance to invoke the criminal
law and impose a penalty. Thus in regulating contracts and combinations in restraint of trade, we
began with criminal prosecutions. Then, for a sea-
son we relied upon dissolution suits in equity. Today
administrative action of the Federal Trade Commission has become our chief reliance. A like story
might be told with respect to factory acts, housing

laws, traffic regulations, or, indeed, almost any recently developed field of legal control.

Of the four ways of sanctioning legal precepts, punishment and substitutional redress are the oldest and the least satisfactory. Punishment ought to be reserved for the criminal law. But all experience has shown that criminal law should not be used as the everyday agency for every sort of case, but should be reserved for the direct and immediate maintaining of the general security and the general morals against types of anti-social individual and of anti-social conduct. The modern forms of sanction are specific redress and prevention.

Development of prevention as a legal remedy, has only begun. We have not gone much further than interference by injunction to prevent immediately threatened physical infringements of economic claims, and, in recent years, to prevent interference with the nation-wide economic functions which are under the protection of the federal government. In England, injunctions are used to prevent defamation, and there is an increasing tendency in this country to use them to protect personality. But the deeper possibilities of prevention have received scant attention from lawyers. Yet it seems clear that preventive justice will play a large part in the law of the future. The prejudice against it in the minds of common-law lawyers is historical in origin and has no sound basis.

Reference has been made to the growth of administrative justice which has gone forward so rapidly in the present century. But the circumstances which call for administration call no less for preventive justice. Indeed, administration is one of the chief means of preventive justice, and the most effective work in the way of prevention that goes on in our legal order today is done through administration. The industrial society of today demands legislation to make clear what may be done and what not, and demands administration to guide men away from conflict and controversy, in preference to elaborate judicial investigation and exact reparation after injury. Legislation does for conduct in many fields what the lines in the middle of the road and the lines upon the street crossings do for the driver of the automobile. Administration does for an increasing number of activities what the traffic officer at the corner does both for automobile driver and for pedestrian. The efficacy of the work of the traffic officer is in the individualized nature of his directions, as compared with generalized legal precepts. Our economic order requires an individualization in the handling of many things which was not needed in the simpler, rural, agricultural society of the past. When the points of contact between men are relatively few, the general lines and rough compromises drawn and expressed in rules of law suffice for the exigencies of justice. When the points of contact are enormously multiplied, as in the metropolitan city of today, and individual claims conflict and overlap on all sides, it is necessary to have fine lines and delicate discriminations which are not easily made by means of rules of law.

General rules are made through elimination of the particular circumstances and fixing of the common circumstances in a series of cases. In the law of property and in commercial law, this method of elimination and generalization suffices to give a practicable rule. But elimination of circumstances in order to get a rule makes the rule impossible as a self-sufficient practical compromise between the claims of the several participants in the infinitely variable situations involved in human conduct. As the points of contact involved in conduct become more numerous, and the friction of that contact becomes more acute, individualization in the legal treatment of conduct begins to encroach upon the domain of legal rules. This need of individualization is met for judicial justice by means of legal standards, that is, legally defined measures of conduct to be applied with reference to the particular circumstances of each case.

In framing standards, the law seeks neither to generalize by eliminating the features of particular cases, nor to particularize by including them. Instead it seeks to formulate the general expectation of society as to how individuals will act in the course of their undertakings, and thus to guide the common sense of a jury or expert intuition of a board, when called upon to judge of particular conduct under particular circumstances. Titles to property, and the qualities and incidents of commercial paper do not depend, and ought not to depend, on circumstances.   Such matters are governed by rules, which attach definite, detailed legal consequences to definite, detailed states of fact.   Such rules are not left to juries or commissions.   The facts being ascertained, they are applied by a mechanical, logical process. On the other hand, what is due care in driving cannot be determined in the abstract, once for all, for every driver who will ever drive.   In cases of this sort the modern law resorts not to rules but to legal standards devised to guide tribunals in applying to each unique set of circumstances their common sense resulting from their experience.   But this device of standards, which has proved so useful in the law of torts, in equity, and above all, in the law of public utilities, is not available, or is available only within narrow limits, in criminal law.   The exigencies of the general security preclude resort to it.   The policy which led our federal courts and so many of our states to reject common-law misdemeanors, and led in Continental Europe to the doctrine *nulla poena sine lege*, no penalty without a rule of law, forbids our doing in criminal law what is done through standards in so many fields of civil justice.

Legal standards are the judicial response to the need of individualization, as the setting up of administrative tribunals and increasing reliance upon administration is the legislative response thereto.   Each is ultimately a response to the conditions of an urban, industrial society and to a complicated economic order resting on a minute division of labor.   The same conditions that brought each into existence are making and must make for a greater development of preventive justice.

Our historical common law had very little in the way of preventive machinery. There was a crude preventive device in the jurisdiction of criminal tribunals or of magistrates to put a threatening offender under bond to keep the peace. There was an old real action, long obsolete, by which to obtain a judicial declaration that one who claimed a servitude in another's land had no such right. Later, courts of equity developed a jurisdiction to enjoin threatened injuries to property rights and to construe trusts and advise trustees as to their duties. That is as far as our law had gone until quite recently. In countries governed by the Roman law the development of preventive remedies on the civil side of the law has gone much further than with us. In England today one who claims to be interested in a deed or will or other written instrument may obtain a judicial interpretation and judicial declaration of his rights. Declaratory-judgment legislation has been urged by bar associations in this country, and a few states have adopted statutes modeled on the English practice. Likewise the gradual but persistent and continual enlargement of the power of courts of equity to grant injunctions and the continually growing use of injunctions as a means of police, indicate a movement to extend the most effective of the preventive remedies developed in the past. Obviously preventive justice on this side of the law is gaining ground. More-

over, with the setting up of modern municipal courts
in our larger cities, we have begun to devise bureaus
of justice, to which the citizen may resort in order
to know his rights, instead of leaving him to guess at
them at his peril, and then judging his conduct *ex
post facto*.   But this cautious development of preventive justice on the civil side of the law, significant
as it is of the direction of legal development for the
future, is but a small part of the matter.   It leaves
untouched the great field of criminal law, a field in
which, more than anywhere else, preventive justice
might be made to achieve great things.

Substantially all of the energies of our elaborate
punitive justice are devoted to dealing with offenders
after the offense.   The police are, indeed, an agency
of prevention.   But they are chiefly an agency of
forcible prevention at the crisis of action.   Juvenile
courts have done much incidentally in the way of a
preventive activity directed to the ultimate causes of
delinquency.   Our agencies of probation and parole,
struggling with many adverse conditions and (in
most jurisdictions, at least) laboring under burdens
of defective organization and insufficient equipment,
have nevertheless done something in the same direction.   Yet making full allowance for these things, it
remains true that our legal treatment of delinquents
is not preventive but is punitive in its conception and
administration.

Our substantive criminal law is based upon a
theory of punishing the vicious will.   It postulates
a free moral agent, confronted with a choice between

doing right and doing wrong, and choosing freely to do wrong. It assumes that the social interest in the general security and the social interest in the general morals are to be maintained by imposing on him a penalty corresponding exactly to the gravity of his offense. It is enforced by an elaborate machinery for exacting the appointed penalty. Parallel to this machinery of detection, conviction, and penal treatment, is a no less elaborate system of mitigating devices, intended to bring about the needed individualization, but affording those who are skilled in working its mechanisms a succession of opportunities for extricating particular delinquents from the clutches of the law. The lawyer's interest is in the machinery of prosecution and conviction and the machinery of mitigation. With what goes on before the commission of an offense, with the conditions that generate offenders and insure a steady grist to the mill of criminal justice, the lawyer is not concerned. His part begins when the morning paper tells him of the committed crime. What goes on before and leads up to the crime, often much more surely and inevitably than the committed crime leads to conviction and the appointed penal treatment, is outside of his domain. Very likely he will tell us that his science has to do with what is, not with what ought to be. The criminal law, he will say, is a body of precepts for the repression of anti-social conduct. Until there is concrete anti-social conduct, it does not come into play. If, within jealously guarded traditional limits, something may be done through legal agencies to reach the causes that lie behind concrete anti-social action, he will say the science of legislation must be appealed to. The science of law, as we had understood it until quite recently, assumes legal precepts as already existent. It does not tell us how to direct our creative energies to the devising of new precepts or of new and improved machinery of making them effective.

A complete change in the spirit and attitude of the science of law has been going forward in the twentieth century. But as yet it has made little impression upon the profession. Such cautious lawmaking as we have had looking toward preventive justice, has commonly met the fate of measures proceeding on ideas unfamiliar to the common-law lawyer, and been pronounced unconstitutional. Not a little in the way of education must precede legislation on this subject, if we are to have enduring results.

In effect, what there is in the way of preventive justice, in the domain of the criminal law, is achieved not by legal but by extra-legal agencies. It is done for the most part not by the agencies of the law, but by social workers. In other words, we have yet to devise the machinery and learn the technique of preventive criminal justice. Much of the little that has been done has been experimental, and some of it, no doubt, has been misdirected. But we can not doubt that the development of preventive justice is destined to be as epoch-making for jurisprudence as the development of preventive medicine has been for medical science.

II

THE DIFFICULTIES OF CRIMINAL JUSTICE

Inherent Difficulties in All Justice According to Law

Law is something more than an aggregate of rules. Hence enforcement of law is much more than applying to definite detailed states of fact the pre-appointed definite detailed consequences. Law must govern life, and the very essence of life is change. No legislative omniscience can predict and appoint consequences for the infinite variety of detailed facts which human conduct continually presents. Indeed, much well meant lawmaking fails of its purpose because it presupposes that it is enough to frame rules and ignores other elements in law which are decisive when the rules come to be applied. Only the most primitive bodies of law are composed wholly of rules, and even in primitive codes there is a certain amount of traditional "interpretation" to be reckoned with. One cause of much popular dissatisfaction with the administration of justice according to law is to be found in the tendency to overlook everything but the rule element in law. But, more than this, each of the elements of which a developed body of law is made up involves a special source of difficulty, arising out of its nature and its relation to the layman's ideas of justice and of what the law ought to achieve.

In a highly organized society, three elements go to make up the law, namely, first, a body of legal precepts, second, a traditional technique of finding the grounds of decision for particular cases in that body of precepts and of developing, interpreting, and applying those precepts to meet new and unforeseen states of fact, and, third, a body of received ideals of the social and legal order, of what law is for and hence of what legal precepts should be both in their substance and in their application. The precept element is made up of rules, principles, conceptions, and standards—that is, of rules prescribing definite detailed results for definite detailed states of fact, of generalized authoritative starting points for legal reasoning when detailed facts are presented which do not wholly correspond to those presupposed by the rules, of generalized situations of fact into which the facts of particular cases may be classified by legal reasoning so as to determine what rules apply, and of formulated measures of conduct, to be applied with reference to the special circumstances of the case in hand. This precept element involves difficulties in the administration of justice according to law whether we look at one of its forms or at another. As has been said in another connection, rules are framed by a process of generalization and elimination which may very likely cast out of account the unique features of some particular case which for that case, in its special circumstances, may be relevant to a proper weighing of all the claims to be adjusted. Thus the mechanical working of the rule, important from the standpoint of the general security, may be unsatisfactory from the standpoint of the individual life. Principles are formulated by still higher generalizations and consequent elimination of still more of the special facts of particular cases. Thus they may easily reject considerations which seem to the layman controlling and give the administration of justice according to law an artificial and mechanical appearance. Also conceptions are framed for the generality of cases. In consequence it may be necessary to fit to them by the method of Procrustes cases which are out of the ordinary. On the civil side of the law the need of individualization, which arises from these characteristics of legal precepts in their application, is met by means of standards. But, as has been seen, standards are inapplicable in criminal justice, or at least are applicable only within narrow and jealously guarded limits.

For the most part in criminal law we have to do with rules; and the most constant and most universal cause of dissatisfaction with law grows out of the mechanical operation of legal rules. A balance between rules of law and magisterial discretion, which will give effect both to the general security and the individual life, with the least impairment of either, is perhaps the most difficult problem of the science of law.

For centuries it has been sought to administer justice now by rules exclusively or chiefly, and now chiefly by discretion. Such attempts have never succeeded. But the fact that they have been made so repeatedly and persistently shows that we have to do with an inherent difficulty. There is seldom an even balance. For the most part, the administration of justice has swung back and forth from an extreme reliance upon the one to a no less extreme reliance upon the other. In the strict law of the later Middle Ages in England, and in the maturity of American law in the last half of the nineteenth century, the stress was put upon rules. Attempt was made to exclude all individualization and to confine the magistrate to strict observance of minute and detailed precepts, or to a mechanical process of application of law through logical deduction from fixed principles. On the other hand, in the administrative tribunals of sixteenth- and seventeenth-century England, in the executive and legislative justice of the American colonies, and in administrative boards and commissions which have been set up so lavishly in the present century, the stress is put upon discretion and individualization. Here, in contrast, a wide power is given to the magistrate to fit the action of the tribunal to the facts of the individual case. But already some reaction from this administrative justice is manifest. Apparently, the mechanical action of legal rules may be tempered, but we may not hope to obviate it.

As was said in another connection, rules of law are general rules, made by eliminating what experience or reasoning point out as by and large the immaterial elements of particular controversies. So far as cases are alike, and so far as it is possible to foresee or to calculate with reasonable precision the extent to which concrete disputes approximate to the types reached by generalization, the results are good. But in practice cases are by no means all alike, nor do they approximate to the types established by the law in ways admitting of exact prediction or precise measurement. There are endless gradations. Often one type so shades into another that it is difficult to choose with assurance the type to which a given case is to be referred. This is a prolific cause of judicial disagreements. Because of this impossibility of laying out exact limits in advance we can never be sure, when we eliminate what seem the less significant factors in order to frame a general rule, that we are not eliminating something which will have an important bearing on some particular controversy.

In periods when reliance is put upon strict law, the desire to eliminate discretion leads to attempt to meet the demands of exceptional cases by an elaborate apparatus of exceptions to rules and of qualifications and detailed provisos. In the latter part of the eighteenth century it was believed that reason was equal to the task of meeting with an appropriate legislative provision every case which could arise. As might have been expected, however, such ambitious codes have uniformly come to nought. No lawmaker has been able to foresee more than the broad outlines of the clash of interests or more than the main lines of the courses of conduct to which the law even of his own time must be applied. Moreover, a legal system which seeks to cover everything by a special provision becomes cumbrous and unworkable.

As discretion cannot be wholly eliminated, the tendency is to provide some mechanism for controlling it, or to seek to subject it to rules. A certain judicial or magisterial dispensing power will be found in every body of law, and in developed legal systems there is usually a series of devices for introducing discretion into the administration of justice. Our criminal justice has a long series of such devices. The police exercise a certain discretion as to who shall be brought before the tribunals. The public prosecutor has wide and substantially uncontrolled power of ignoring offenses or offenders, of dismissing proceedings in their earlier stages, of so presenting them to grand juries that no indictment follows, of declining to prosecute after indictment, and of agreeing to accept a plea of guilty of a lesser offense. The grand jury may ignore a charge and refuse to find an indictment. The trial jury notoriously exercises a dispensing power through its general verdict of not guilty. The court has at common law wide discretion as to sentence, and often as to suspension or mitigation of sentence. In recent years we have added probation and parole; and at the top of the series is the executive's prerogative of pardon. Some of these are hedged about with procedural limitations. But such limitations, if they are effective to restrain what might otherwise be an intolerable margin for the personal equation of the official, are very likely to give these devices a purely mechanical operation and thus afford opportunity for perversion of the legal provision for special cases into a means of enabling the typical offender to escape.

Thus far the law has been able to do no more than achieve a practical compromise between over-minute law-making and over-wide discretion. In consequence, some sacrifice of flexibility of application to particular cases is inevitable, and this sacrifice is sure to entail occasional injustice. Moreover, it gives to rules of law an arbitrary appearance and not infrequently makes the application of law run counter to the moral ideas of individual citizens. This is especially true in times of transition. Wherever there are strong conflicting interests or divergent ideals of justice and whenever groups or classes are asserting claims which do not admit of easy reconciliation, there is likely to be vigorous complaint of the want of accord of law with the individual moral sense. For the individual looks only at single cases and measures them by his individual sense of right and wrong. The courts must look at cases with respect to types and classifications and must measure them by a generalized, and hence to some extent artificial, standard. We fear to give the judge wide discretion lest, even in the best of judges, his exercise of it reflect the desires of the element of society in which he was reared, or with which he associates. But if we tie his hands by rules of law, he may be bound to apply mechanically the ethical ideas of a past generation as formulated in common law and legislation. Whichever course we take, it is certain that judicial standards and the standards of individual critics, both applied in the best of faith, will diverge seriously. This is a fruitful and universal cause of popular dissatisfaction with the administration of justice.

Difficulties and causes of dissatisfaction inhere in the technique element of law because of lack of popular appreciation of the need and value of an authoritative technique. It seems enough to provide rules. It is not perceived readily that the life of a rule is in its application, and that it is quite as important that the process of application be certain as that the rule itself be certain. In a democracy, especially, the public is not unlikely to underestimate the difficulties in application of law, to assume that any one is competent to fit a rule to a case, or at least, that any one is competent to criticize the process of application in action simply on the basis of such interests as appear on the surface.

In truth expert training or trained experience are required both for the framing of legal precepts and for applying them. Traditional rules of law may be compared to the formulas of engineers. They sum up the experience of generations of judges in many cases and enable one who knows the art of application to apply that experience without having participated in it, just as the formula of the engineer enables him to utilize the accumulated experience of the past, even though he could not of himself work out a step in its evolution. In the case of the judge no less than in that of the engineer there must be special knowledge and special preparation. It is no more possible for any honest man to apply the one formula than the other. On the one hand, the administration of justice suffers from the making or shaping of precepts without adequate grasp of the interests involved and an adequate conception of how to adjust them. On the other hand, it suffers from application of legal precepts without adequate perception that application of them is a technical art requiring to be mastered. Not infrequently an application which does no more than employ the established common-law technique is criticized as judicial usurpation because it departs from the letter. There was a striking example of this some years ago when the Supreme Court of the United States did no more than apply received canons of interpretation to the anti-trust laws. At other times, when the courts refuse to go beyond what the authoritative technique permits, they are accused of mechanical and pedantic literalness. There were many examples of this during the agitation for recall of judges and recall of judicial decisions in the first and second decades of the present century.

We have inherited from pioneer America a faith in versatility; a confidence that any man is equal to anything. This faith is stronger in some parts of the land than in others. But very generally, in the form of a feeling that any one is as competent to understand what justice requires in the intricate controversies and complicated relations of an urban industrial society, as he may have been to understand

it in the simpler disputes and simpler relations of an
agricultural society, it leads to impatience or suspicion of proper standards of training for the bar, to
low standards of qualification for judicial office, and
to something like contempt for scientific methods and
a high measure of technical skill.   The influence of
this faith in versatility may be seen in most of the
states of the South and West in extravagant powers
of juries, in lay judges of probate, and in legislative
or judicial attacks upon the doctrine of precedents.
In criminal law it is usually manifest in legislation
committing the fixing of penalties to trial juries.
But it should be added that more than one cause
has led to such legislation in different parts of the
country.

It is worth while to emphasize that the public has
a deep and direct interest in maintaining the highest
scientific standards in the administration of justice.
This is by no means generally realized.   But when
we complain, as we do constantly, of American judicial justice in comparison with that of the rest of the
world, we need to reflect on the requirements for participation in the application and enforcement of law
which we maintain or tolerate, in comparison with
those which obtain elsewhere in industrial societies,
and on the training, organization, and mode of
selection of those to whom we commit the machinery
of criminal justice, in comparison with other lands.
Our traditional reliance is on publicity.   But public
indignation may be invoked only in extreme cases.
It cannot be an everyday guarantee of efficient work-

ing of the institutions of justice. Nor is it always called forth in the right cases. For the ordinary workings of justice we must rely rather on the expert criticism of a well-trained bar. The knowledge that nothing which does not conform to the principles and received doctrines of the law will escape the notice of the bar, can do more than any other agency for the proper and efficient operation of the courts. But, as things are in our large cities today, it happens too often that the lawyers who are chiefly conversant with what goes on in criminal tribunals scrutinize it from a radically different standpoint. The best trained element of the bar more and more does its chief work out of court, and almost wholly avoids criminal cases. Thus the most effective check upon the administration of justice becomes inoperative. This special difficulty is added to by and grows out of public reluctance to admit the necessity of scientific justice and the training of the bar, and so of the bench, which it presupposes.

Much of what has been said as to the technique element applies also to the ideal element of law. The received ideals of the law have been reached by generalized experience, given shape by the dominant moral, social, and economic conceptions of the time when the ideals on any given subject crystallized. In contrast, the ideals by which laymen judge of the law in action are likely to be reached on the basis of particular situations in which all the relevant factors, in a large view, are by no means sure to be included. In criminal law, particularly, a judge imposing sentence must go thoroughly into the details of the conditions, internal and external, under which an act was done. He must look into the motive of the act and its consequences. The legal ideal is one of exact adjustment of the penalty to the particular case by way of compensation for the generality of the legal precept which was applied mechanically in determining conviction. Popular judgments in such cases are likely to be reached by labeling acts according to certain obvious consequences, in which event there is demand for a stereotyped sentence ignoring all consideration of the individual accused. But they are quite as likely at other times to be reached by looking solely at the personality of the accused. In that event, there is demand for a dispensing power before conviction. Thus although judge and lay critic might agree on the ultimate moral standard to be applied in a particular case, their conclusions may be far apart. The public are apt to assume that this disagreement argues defects in the administration of justice, and American criminal justice has suffered from that assumption. On the one hand, we have continual legislation infringing on or taking away discretion in sentencing, and on the other hand, legislation giving extravagant powers to juries so as to promote a dispensing power.

A more prolific cause of dissatisfaction, inherent in the ideal element of law, grows out of the difference in rate of progress between an authoritative professional tradition and a more fluid lay public opinion. The ideal element in law does change, as one may see by comparing the ideals of a relationally organized society, which still obtain in our classical seventeenth-century law books, with the ideals of a competitive individualistic society, which control in the law books of the nineteenth century. But they change slowly, and in those parts of the law which have to do with the security of acquisitions and the economic organization of society very slowly. Not infrequently, especially in times of transition, the ideals of the law are those which once obtained in public opinion at large, but do so, or are coming to do so, no longer.

To some extent this difficulty exists also with respect to the precept element. So far as legal precepts are formulations of public opinion, they cannot be framed until public opinion has become reasonably fixed and settled, and cannot well change until public opinion has definitely changed. It follows that legal precepts are almost certain to lag behind public opinion whenever the latter is active and growing. But detailed legal precepts are easily changed. Indeed, in America, on the average, their life is short. What really lags behind public opinion, and in so doing gives rise to dissatisfaction with the administration of justice, is the element of received ideals. This element controls the interpretation and application of precepts, and often retards or renders nugatory attempts to change precepts by legislative action.

Many devices have been resorted to in order to make the law more immediately sensitive and responsive to public opinion. In America, we have relied much on frequent and copious legislation upon legal subjects, so much so that in many jurisdictions it is far from easy to keep informed as to the state of the statute law. In the fore part of the last century, in different degrees in different parts of the country, we tried deprofessionalizing the practice of law by opening it to all, regardless of education and special training, putting of the courts into politics by making judges elective, often for short terms, and conferring wide powers upon juries at the expense of courts. More than one jurisdiction carried some or all of these to extremes. Each had the effect of enfeebling our criminal justice, and public opinion today is beginning to demand that some of them be given up in order that these devices, meant to make judicial justice responsive to public opinion, shall not keep it wholly out of touch therewith. In the present century we have relied chiefly on the setting up of administrative tribunals with large jurisdiction to be exercised in a non-technical fashion. Few, if any, of these tribunals, however, have succeeded in maintaining any automatic adjustment to public opinion, and more than one, in action, has subjected the administration of justice not to public opinion but to influences destructive of the interests which law seeks to maintain. Other devices urged in the present century are recall of judges and recall of judicial decisions. But these have not commended themselves to the country at large, since they involve obvious menace to the general security.

We must recognize that this difficulty in justice according to law may be minimized, but not wholly obviated. We can do no more than achieve a practical compromise. Public opinion is seldom so definite, so clearly ascertainable in matters of detail, or so unanimous, as to be suffered to be applied directly upon those who administer the law. It must rather affect the administration of justice indirectly through pressure upon those who frame the precepts by which tribunals are governed and by shaping the ideals of those who sit in the tribunals. But if public opinion affects the action of tribunals through the precepts by which they decide and the ideals by which those precepts are interpreted, developed and applied, as the precepts, once established, stand till abrogated or altered and ideals, once received, obtain until new ones are definitely set up and become a part of the authoritative tradition, it follows that the law will not respond quickly to new conditions. It will not be likely to change until ill effects are felt. Indeed, our experience with criminal law suggests that there will be little thoroughgoing change until ill effects are felt acutely. The economic or political or moral change must come first. While it is coming, and until it is so definite and complete as to affect both legal precepts and received ideals and formulate itself in each, divergence between law and a growing public opinion is likely to become acute and to create public dissatisfaction. We must pay this price for the certainty and uniformity demanded by the economic order. Yet it must be conceded that over-solicitude for the general security led lawyers in the last century to give too much weight to the demand for certainty and uniformity. They sometimes spoke of them as things to be sought at any price. They sometimes wrote as if divergence between law and morals, between received legal ideals and public opinion, were merits in the legal system instead of occasional unhappy necessities. We must be careful not to let our consciousness of this inherent difficulty lead us to neglect the task of reducing this difference in rate of growth between law and public opinion wherever and so far as possible.

Another source of difficulty in enforcing law and of dissatisfaction with the administration of justice according to law is involved in human nature. Law is an agency of social control, achieving its task through the force of politically organized society. It prescribes restraint, or, as it has been put, "life measured by reason." It adjusts relations and regulates conduct with at least a threat of force always in the background. In an urban, industrial society, as we have seen, there is of necessity an enormous increase in the amount of restraint and adjustment and regulation. But however necessary or salutary they may be, men are not easily reconciled to them. Many American communities are still so close to the frontier, in point of time and traditions, and modes of thought, that the characteristic pioneer hostility to discipline, good order, and obedience is likely to be latent even in the better class of citizens. The restraint which the law imposes is almost always to some degree a compromise between each individual and his fellows. In eras of authority, these compromises may be accepted by people at large without much question. In times when authority is challenged, and especially in times and places in which absolute democratic theories obtain, they are likely to be scrutinized jealously by the individual who is required to abate some of his activities in the interest of his fellows. The maximum of individual free self-assertion being taken to be the highest good, men are not unlikely to apply that measure concretely with reference to their own desires rather than abstractly, subsuming their desires under a generalization which includes those of their fellows. Also the feeling that each man, as an organ of the sovereign democracy, is in some sense above the law which he helps to make, fosters impatience of legal methods, disrespect for legal institutions, and even a spirit of resistance to them. Such things make administration of justice according to law the more difficult the more we resort to law as the chief agency of social control. They insure that, whether or not the precepts of the law are enforced, dissatisfaction will result.

In the United States these difficulties growing out of human impatience of restraint are aggravated further by political and legal theories of "natural law" inherited from the eighteenth century. The founders of our polity believed in a "natural right of revolution" and argued that conformity to the dictates of the individual conscience was the test of the validity of a law. Ideas of this sort permeate our classical political and juristic writings. In our pioneer communities, where the common defence was the most pressing phase of the general security, they did no harm and, on the other hand, did much good in leading to critical examination of the precepts and institutions, often shaped for a different social order, which had come over from the old world. But their echoes today do not make for an effective legal order. To take some examples a few years old, which do not draw us into the controversies of the moment, consider the declaration of Mr. Gompers, in a Labor Day address two decades ago, that he would not obey mandates of the courts which deprived him of his "natural rights." Consider the pronouncement of a well-known preacher a decade ago that the trouble was not lawlessness, but the enactment of legislation at variance with the "law of nature." Consider the addresses of public officials a decade ago commending administrative violation of the legal rights of certain obnoxious persons as meeting the views of law-abiding citizens whose will, I suppose, had the force of law. Consider that one of the law officers of the federal government not much more than a decade ago, publicly approved mob violence toward such persons, apparently, as an exercise by the rioters of their natural authority to dispense with the law. In the same spirit juries have been wont to take their power of rendering general verdicts as a warrant for disregarding statutes in the utmost good faith. Perhaps the extreme example is to be seen in the repeated acquittals in the Sunday closing prosecutions in Chicago in 1908, although the law of Illinois in a measure invited such things by making jurors judges of the law. But one may see less extreme cases anywhere at any time. It is not easy for the respect for law, demanded by the general security in an urban, industrial society, to flourish in such an atmosphere.

The Antinomy of Criminal Justice

Thus far we have considered difficulties and causes of popular dissatisfaction which affect the whole administration of justice, both civil and criminal. In addition, there are difficulties and causes of dissatisfaction peculiar to criminal law. Perhaps the most deep rooted and universal of these difficulties arises immediately from the history of this branch of the law. But it is intimately connected with the task of the criminal law and, indeed, with the task of social control through organized society. It grows out of a condition of internal contradiction, which goes back to the historical origins of the system of precepts imposing absolute duties and enforced through penalties. It might be called the antinomy of criminal justice.

Historically, criminal law begins in legal regulation of certain crude, pre-legal forms of social control. One of these points of origin is a religious institution of sacrificing an impious wrongdoer to an offended god, who might else inflict his wrath upon the whole community. Lest the community be involved in his guilt, the evil man, whose impiety was offensive to the gods, was put away. Another point of origin is in community self-help. In Germanic law, when a serious crime was committed, the hue and cry was raised and the neighbors turned out armed and blowing horns, to chase the offender. If they caught him, he was dispatched summarily, after the manner of lynch law. Similarly, in the beginnings of the Roman polity, the plebeians were wont to throw an offender from the Tarpeian rock. In part, also, the authority of the state to punish is derived historically from the conception of the king as "father of his country." The king's jurisdiction over the individual member of the community comes down from the authority of the head of a patriarchal household. Another point of origin is in self-help on the part of the person injured and his kinsmen. The beginnings of law are more concerned to regulate and so far as possible obviate the resulting private war than to restrain wrongdoing. Orderly retaliation is the staple of primitive codes. For a long time tort and crime are not differentiated. At Rome down to the Twelve Tables there was capital punishment in what might be called private suits. Indeed, in theory the staple remedy for what we should call a tort was a money penalty. Still another point of origin is to be found in the disciplinary power of the military commander. Thus the Roman magistrate had *imperium*, i.e., power to command the citizen to the end of preserving order in time of peace and discipline in time of war. Essentially this was a military conception, since war was the normal condition of an ancient community. The military chief was more and more invested with what we should call civil jurisdiction as the development of organized society gave rise to new duties and demanded new means of enforcing them. Lastly, there is a point of origin in what comes to be legislation. When legislation, adjudication, and administration were undifferentiated, an *ex post facto* law and execution thereof by a popular assembly, or by its committee, was a step forward in the development of criminal law out of lynch law. To put it summarily, we may say that the historical origins of the criminal law are in sacrificial execution, in offhand popular vengeance, in patriarchal paternal power, in private self-help, in magisterial discipline, and in legislative justice.

Difficulties with which it is still beset are involved in a certain common element in the evolution of a legal social control from these primitive materials. With the rise of social control through politically organized society, religious devotion of the offender to the offended gods became outlawry, and religious sacrificial execution became legal execution. The law began to regulate the occasions and the manner of such outlawings and executings, and to prescribe in detail the formal steps leading thereto. The patriarchal king became a chief magistrate with powers fixed and limited by law. The institution of mob self-help acquired a legal character in that legal limitations were imposed upon it, and it was subjected to legal ceremonials. Private penalties and ransom from private vengeance grew into civil liability to repair damage, leaving punishment to the field of public justice. The disciplinary power of the magistrate was subjected to legal limitations, and the precepts imposing these limitations became the criminal law. Also the legislative committees became courts, and legislative justice was succeeded by judicial justice. Thus criminal law, as conditioned by its origin and history, has a twofold nature. On the one hand, it is made up of commands and prohibitions addressed to the individual in order to secure social interests. On the other hand, it is made up of limitations upon the enforcement of those commands and prohibitions in order to secure the individual life. The part which issues orders to the citizen is futile without magisterial action to give it effect. But magisterial action to make it effective is held down by the part addressed to the magistrate.

This condition of internal opposition is imposed upon criminal law by its history. But it is in some measure inseparable from the task of criminal justice. Criminal law involves the most insistent and most fundamental of social interests. On the one hand, civilized society presupposes peace and good order, security of social institutions, security of the general morals, and conservation and intelligent use of social resources. But on the other hand, and no less, it presupposes free individual initiative, as the basis of economic progress, free criticism, as a condition of political progress, free mental activity, as a prerequisite of cultural progress. Above all, it demands that the individual man be able to live a moral

and social life as a human being. These claims,
which we generalize as the social interest in the individual life, continually trench upon the interest in the
security of social institutions. Often, at least in appearance, they conflict with the paramount interest
in the general security. A wise compromise becomes
very difficult when it has to be made by means of
generalized formulas and to be applied more or less
mechanically.

With us, the broader lines of this compromise are
laid down in bills of rights embodied in our constitutions, and much impatience with more than one of the
guarantees in these bills of rights is manifest in all
recent projects for the overhauling of criminal procedure. But these guarantees are a response to a
fundamental and universal problem of human nature.
Self-assertion and the will to power, desire to do
things freely and desire to dominate over the doings
and control the actions of others, are deep rooted
tendencies of humanity which require government
and law, if civilization is to be maintained and go forward. Yet they make government and its legal
agencies dangerous to the very interests they exist to
maintain and further. We must utilize the will to
power as an instrument for ordered life in society.
But we must hold it in, lest it go beyond the demands
of life ordered by reason and impair free individual
self-assertion beyond the inevitable minimum.

From this need of ordering by masterful rulers
and equal need of confining the masterful rulers to
the purposes for which rule is ordained, two rival

systems have developed—the régime of administration and the régime of law. The former emphasizes efficient rule, the latter emphasizes spontaneous individual initiative and free individual action. The former emphasizes official doing of things, the latter stresses private doing of things. The former looks chiefly to an executive hierarchy, the latter gives the primacy to a judicial hierarchy. The former relies on guidance through experienced direction, the latter on trial and error through experience of decision. The former would hold down the will to power through organization and allocation of definite work to each official, by marking out the domain of each, and by inspection and supervision through administrative superiors. The latter would hold down the will to power through subjecting every official and every official act to the law of the land applied after trial and reasoned argument in a judicial proceedings. The former postulates a wise ruler or wise group of rulers, governed by enlightened motives and possessed of energy, integrity, and good will. The latter postulates a fundamental law and a widespread and deep seated determination to abide it. The former keeps up the tradition of imperial Rome. It succeeds to the Byzantine emperor and the French king of the old régime, and puts a sovereign people and its ministers and officers where the Roman polity put the emperor and his officials, and the old French polity put the king and his ministers and agents. The latter keeps up the Germanic or medieval tradition of the king ruling "under God and the law." It thinks of a sovereign people, its lawmaking bodies, its executives and its judges alike, as under the law of the land. But this law of the land is a body of limitations and checks; a body of guarantees of individual liberties. For our bills of rights are really bills of liberties. They do not guarantee to us any specific claims against our neighbors. They assure us margins of legal non-restraint of our natural powers.

Thus one part of the modern world has taken the line of stress upon efficient enforcing institutions. The other part, and we in America have gone furthest in that part, has taken the line of stress upon a large guaranteed margin of non-interference, even at the expense of efficient guarantees of the general security. It is significant that in more than one quarter of Continental Europe there is renewed interest in the declarations of the rights of man, while in this country, since the beginning of the present century, there has been restiveness with respect to our bills of rights.

As a result of the conflict between these interests, legal history shows a continual movement back and forth between extreme solicitude for the general security and extreme solicitude for the individual life. The one leads to a minimum of regard for the individual accused and to reliance upon summary, unhampered, arbitrary, administrative punitive justice. The other leads to a minimum of regard for the general security and the security of social institutions, and to reliance upon strictly regulated judicial punitive justice, hampered at all points by checks and balances and technical obstacles. Within the memory of the present generation, we have seen an extreme of sentimental tenderness toward accused persons, and a reaction to callousness toward elementary human rights and Draconian severity. In this familiar contrast may be seen in miniature a picture of what has always gone on in the history of criminal law. In penal treatment, it is a movement back and forth between severity and humanity. In law it is a movement back and forth between emphasis on substance and emphasis on procedure.

Inherent Difficulties in Criminal Justice

It remains to note certain general difficulties for which allowance must be made in any appraisal of the criminal justice of a time or place. Some of these difficulties are in the very subject matter of criminal law. They inhere in all attempts to order human conduct and adjust human relations by any system of prosecution and penal treatment through legal or administrative machinery which the wit of man has been able to set up. Other difficulties have their roots in the time in which a given body of criminal law is administered. Such difficulties are wider than the place which we may be considering. They are involved in the social and economic conditions of the time. They grow out of the ideas of the end or purpose of law held generally in that time, and the general attitude of the time toward law and government. We must give first place among these difficulties to one which must be taken into account in every field of the law, but is especially operative in criminal law, namely, the inherent limitations on effective legal action. No legal machinery of which we have any knowledge is equal to doing everything which we might like to achieve through social control by law. Some duties which morally are of the highest moment are yet too intangible for legal enforcement. This is brought out in the experience of domestic relations courts, and juvenile courts, which continually have to take over the methods and aims and point of view of administrative rather than of judicial tribunals. In no other cases is self-redress so persistently resorted to, nor so likely to be approved by the public, as in cases of disturbing the integrity or the peace of a household. But the futility of legal interference in many of the commonest forms of such disturbance has been shown by abundant experience and is generally recognized. For the modes of inflicting injury often are too subtle to be reached by the machinery of legal precept and prosecution, and the legal alternative, preventive remedies, may involve intolerable interference with individual liberty. There are a few cases in which the would-be wrecker of a family has been enjoined. There is nothing, however, to indicate that these injunctions had any results beyond contempt proceedings and appeals. Likewise, many cases involve serious and undoubted wrongs to individuals and yet may be too small for the ponderous and expensive machinery of prosecution. How to deal with the small annoyances and neighborhood quarrels and petty depredations and small-scale predatory activities which irritate the mass of an urban population, but do not seem to involve enough to justify the costly process of the law, is by no means the least of the problems of justice in the modern city.

Thus much wrong goes on with which law cannot deal. But when we come to the wrongs with which it can deal, we still encounter the obstacle that legal precepts, however wisely chosen and skilfully framed, will not enforce themselves. We must rely upon individuals to set the legal machinery in motion. We must in some way stimulate them to go to the trouble of vindicating the law, and how much trouble that may involve, Mr. Arthur Train has portrayed vividly in his story of the cook and the teapot. Where so much in the way of time and inconvenience and even annoyance is demanded, we must be careful not to discourage those who know of committed crimes from coming forward. Yet we must not suffer the criminal law to be used as a means of extortion or of gratifying spite. Legal systems have worked over this dilemma for centuries without attaining a wholly satisfactory result.

Next to the limitations on effective legal action, we must put certain difficulties involved in administering the criminal law in a popular government. Continental writers on criminal law have remarked a relaxation of criminal justice which followed the liberal movement in Europe after 1848. The jury has by no means been a satisfactory feature in Continental criminal procedure. It was introduced as a popular institution during the democratic trend of the last century. Its most conspicuous effect has been to bring in an element of dispensing with the law or of mitigating penalties in particular cases which has been no less noticeable in American criminal justice. I have spoken in another connection of popular impatience of restraint, absolute political theories of popular lawmaking, and ideas of the consent of the governed and of natural law, as they affect respect for law. Naïve political theories of popular sovereignty have been shown to have had much to do with fostering the practice of lynching. Without going into controversial matters of the present, one need but read the discussions of the era of Rooseveltian progressivism to see that business men have been known to regard as entirely legitimate evasion of statutes which interfered with their carrying on business as they chose. We must not overlook these phenomena when we are considering disrespect for law at the bottom of the social scale, where it takes cruder, more direct, and less subtle forms. It cannot be denied that we pay a certain price for the advantages of our democratic polity. Respect for law seems to suffer when it is felt widely that law proceeds from the governed and is something which they may make and unmake at their pleasure. The spectacle of forty-eight legislative mills turning out a huge biennial, or even annual, grist of laws makes legal precepts seem transient things. It deprives them of the majesty and solemnity which attached to traditional legal precepts of supposed immemorial antiquity, or even to enactments of the king in parliament, made with pomp and circumstance on rare occasions.   No doubt there is a fallacy in not distinguishing between law and laws.   But it is a fallacy which readily escapes notice.   Those who feel that laws are but expressions or formulations of their will, and are accustomed to seeing those formulations go forward in the offhand way which characterizes much of our state legislation, are not unlikely to assume that what they take to be true of laws is equally true of law.

In a popular government, the close connection of criminal law and the administration of criminal justice with politics, which is another inherent obstacle to enforcement of law, has an especially bad influence.   It must be remembered that criminal law has a much closer connection with politics than has the civil side of the law.   Civil litigation can seldom be used for political ends.   But it is a common experience that criminal prosecutions may have partisan politics behind them, and out of this experience has arisen a fear of oppression through the criminal law which has been no mean factor in American legal history.   Moreover, there have been examples, even in recent times, of drastic enforcement of severe penal laws in order to keep a people or a class in subjection. No small element in our population is made up of emigrants from countries where criminal law has been used in this way, and they have reinforced a tradition brought over by the seventeenth-century immigrants, who had suffered from penal laws directed against their religious views and forms of worship. Nor may it be denied that the power of a majority or even a plurality, in a popular government, to visit with punishment practices which a strong minority, or an easy-going majority, consider in no way objectionable, is capable of abuse. Moreover, we must recognize that criminal prosecutions are possible weapons of offense and defense in class and industrial conflicts. In consequence, whenever such conflicts are in the air, a strain is put upon criminal law and its administration. Suspicion arises that the one side or the other may get an advantage through control of the prosecuting or the judicial machinery. Hence the public has, in the past, been reluctant to give either to prosecutor or to judge the powers and the discretion which each ought to have. Thus the maintenance of the general security is neglected and the atmosphere of criminal prosecutions becomes political. When the public conscience is active, or when public indignation is aroused, prosecution is likely to be spectacular rather than efficient. When the public conscience is sluggish, or when public attention is turned in other directions, prosecuting agencies, subjected to politics, are likely to be lax for fear of offending politicians or dominant or militant political groups.

At the same time, the close connection of criminal law with politics in a democratic government leads to a tendency to put an over-heavy burden upon the criminal law. It has been said that "the capital fact

in the mechanism of modern states is the energy of
the legislature." Popular feeling that law is an expression of the general will, and that what a majority
desires for the moment needs only formal expression
in a legislative act in order to become law, leads to
habitual resort to enacted law when things do not go
as they should. One who points out some defect in
our polity, civil or criminal, is expected to come forward also with the remedy in the form of a statute.
But it is by no means always true that a statute can
provide the remedy. Many unhappy features of our
criminal justice lie too deep to be reached by statutes.
Some of them are due to statutes. Many more have
been aggravated by statutes. Moreover, because of
this habit of turning to legislation on all occasions,
two sorts of lawmaking have become very common
despite their notorious futility. One of these is lawmaking which has nothing behind it but the sovereign
imperative; legislation in which the mere words "be it
enacted" are taken to justify what follows and are
relied upon to bring about the end sought. The
other is lawmaking intended to "educate," that is, to
set up an ideal of what men ought to do rather than
a rule as to what they shall do. However impressive
the state-declared ideal may be to the contemplative
observer, the spectacle of statutory precepts with
penal sanctions, which are not and perhaps are not
intended to be put in force in practice, casts doubt
upon the whole penal code and educates in disrespect
for law more than the high pronouncement can educate for virtue. The enforcement of law depends

largely upon the extent to which the lawmaker can identify social interests with individual interests, and thus enlist individual desire to enforce his precepts. In criminal law, the desire of the offender to escape, and the desire of his friends and relatives that he escape, are strong and active. Unless the desires of other individuals may be enlisted in the service of the law, the agencies of enforcement are likely to fall into an easy-going routine, readily manipulated in the interest of offenders.

Criminal law is the type of law which figures chiefly in the newspapers. Hence when the layman thinks of law, he is almost certain to think of the criminal law. Dickens put his finger on this characteristic of lay ideas about law in portraying Tony Weller. The elder Mr. Weller was clear that the practice of all the courts in the realm was governed by that of the Central Criminal Court at the Old Bailey, and that an alibi, the staple defense at the Old Bailey, was a sovereign specific for a civil action. Also the layman's short and simple cure for all ills, responding to a well known human instinct, is to hurt some one. Mark Twain represents Huck Finn's father, when he stumbled over a barrel, as pausing in his tirade to kick the barrel. Accordingly, when a new measure is to be drafted, the lay lawmaker turns by instinct to the criminal law and every new statute adds at least one more to the mass of prescribed penalties for which a criminal prosecution may be brought. It is hardly possible for any legal machinery to do all which our voluminous penal legisla-

tion expects of it. Even lawyers scarcely appreciate
the operation of the limitations upon all effective
legal action. Thus there is constant pressure upon
the law to "do something," whether it may do anything worth while or not. In periods of transition or
expansion, the tendency is especially strong to call
upon the law to do more than it is adapted to do.
The result is sure to be failure, and failure affects the
whole legal order injuriously. Serious study of how
to make our huge annual output of legislation effective for its purpose without prosecutions is sorely
needed. In general, the sequence is, first, criminal
prosecutions, then, when they achieve nothing, resort
to courts of equity and statutory extensions of the
power of injunction and the drastic and summary
remedy of contempt, and ultimately resort to an administrative commission. Giving up of the naïve
faith in formal lawmaking which finds expression in
the common phrase, "there ought to be a law against
it," would do much for the efficiency of the criminal law.

Regulation of summary community self-help,
through the imposing of limits upon offhand public
vengeance, is one of the earliest forms of criminal
law. The spirit which lay behind this institution of
summary mob self-help in primitive society is still
active. It has its roots in deep seated tendencies of
human behavior, and the administration of justice
has always to reckon with it. Whenever the public
mind is excited, there is a real danger that a criminal
prosecution will become a man hunt, and this danger

is aggravated when newspapers take up the work of criminal investigation, or take a leading part in urging and furthering prosecutions. Recently in the Hall-Mills case in New Jersey we had an example of what prosecutions to furnish news may become. In that case, the accused were persons of means. If they had not been, the results might have been unfortunate. Hence it becomes imperative to impose checks upon the process of criminal investigation, and to set up a guarded criminal procedure in order to preclude, so far as possible, the influence of "mob mind," and, by requiring an indubitable case, demanding deliberation, and prescribing adherence to forms, insure that reason, and not passion and prejudice, determine the judgment. These checks are undoubtedly irksome to those who have to do the work of detection and prosecution. They necessarily interfere to some extent with the effectiveness even of ordinary prosecutions. They are capable of abuse and the professional defenders often take advantage of them to defeat enforcement of the law. But the history of criminal law is full of warnings for those who would do away with these checks. That they are necessary, and yet often a necessary evil, is but another of the inherent difficulties with which the criminal law must contend.

All administration of justice must wrestle with difficulties involved in ascertainment of the facts to which legal precepts must be applied. In primitive law, mechanical modes of trial by ordeal or by casting lots are often resorted to as means of referring an issue of fact to supernatural determination. In our law, an elaborate system of rules of evidence was developed in connection with trial by jury. Lawyers not uncommonly take it to be an organon for the ascertainment of truth. But so regarded, it is little more than a modern form of mechanical trial and appeal to chance. In the English case of Adolf Beck, where an innocent man was twice convicted and served a long term of imprisonment for the crimes of another, the crucial evidence, which would, if gone into, have established Beck's innocence conclusively, was excluded under the rules of evidence as not relevant to the issue. The question as to what is the truth easily becomes lost in critical scrutiny of proceedings at a trial in order to determine whether the technical rules of evidence were or were not observed.

In recent times the progress of psychology has made us aware of the inherent imperfections of human testimony, and has begun to give us some scientific basis for a better organized apparatus of discovering truth. But, except in respect of matters of expert evidence, it is likely to be a long time before we can make much practical use of methods other than those which have grown up in experience of trials, and have been formulated in our law of evidence. In criminal law, where we must reckon not only with the difficulty of discovering offenders, but also with the danger of convicting the innocent, there are special circumstances aggravating the inherent unreliability of evidence. There has been so much palpable escape of the guilty in recent American criminal justice, that we are apt to overlook the very real possibility of conviction of the innocent. The recent case of Slater, released in Scotland and compensated by the government after eighteen years' imprisonment for a murder of which he is now pronounced not to have been guilty, deserves thoughtful consideration by those who would look only at the possibilities of escape of the guilty. We must rely chiefly on human testimony. But criminal trials involve matters with respect to which passions are aroused much more than in civil litigation. Also the consequences are much more serious, and unscrupulous persons are apt to be arrayed on one side or on both. It is a commonplace that errors of observation and unsuspected suggestion affect the testimony of the most conscientious. When passions are aroused, and the unconscientious are before us, the difficulties of proof are multiplied. American lawyers have yet to study scientifically the problem of lying witnesses, defective observation, and suggestion, as affecting proof in criminal cases. The maxims and observations, in which we express our practical experience of these matters under much simpler conditions, are too much of the rule-of-thumb type. They have become little more than pieces to move in the procedural game between prosecutor and accused.

To these general considerations we must add the bad influence of police *esprit de corps*. The unfortunate convictions of Beck in England, which will long remain the classical modern example of conviction of the innocent, were clearly traceable in large part to determination of the police to convict an innocent man whom they honestly but quite erroneously believed to be guilty. Thus they not only overlooked what would have demonstrated Beck's innocence, they were able, and no doubt thought it justifiable, to keep back from prosecutor, counsel for the defense, and the court things making for Beck's innocence which might well have directed attention into the right quarter. The memoirs and reminiscences of experienced trial lawyers contain abundant and uniform testimony to the effect that the evidence of the police is apt to be so colored and warped as to be subject to grave doubt. Indeed, in the Slater case a police officer who was convinced of Slater's innocence and sought to turn the inquiry into the right path was discharged and subjected to an unfounded prosecution. Serjeant Ballantine, whose long experience in prosecuting and defending entitle him to speak with authority, tells us that *esprit de corps*, antipathy towards the criminal classes, the habit of testifying, so that testifying under oath ceases to be regarded as a serious matter, and in particular the temptation which besets police officers to communicate opinions or theories to the press, thus "pledging themselves to views which it is damaging to their sagacity to retract," have caused serious and even fatal miscarriages of justice in Great Britain. Since he wrote, the cases of Beck and Edalji and Slater have reinforced his statements. With us, the cases of Frank and of Stielow tell a like story. Indeed, the student of criminology may verify his conclusions

abundantly from American criminal trials. Yet
from the nature of the case such testimony is the best
available, and in the average case, no doubt, is per-
fectly sound. The difficulty is that we have no adequate means of distinguishing the cases in which it
is infected by the causes enumerated by Serjeant
Ballantine.

Police *esprit de corps* is in some part counteracted
by the activity of habitual defenders of criminals,
and the activity of friends and relatives of the accused. But these are often more available and more
efficacious in the service of the guilty than of the
innocent. Getting witnesses out of the way, or silenc-
ing them, or modifying their testimony by impor-
tunity, social pressure, intimidation, appeals to race
solidarity, or sympathy, are matters thoroughly familiar to the observer of criminal justice in action.
The reminiscences of trial lawyers show that nothing
new in these respects has been devised in the modern
American city. Undoubtedly the securities for individual liberty which surround a common-law prosecution make for a game of wits between the police
and the habitual defenders. But if we put too much
confidence in the police and set our judicial machinery for a task of speedy and assured conviction
of those whom the police bring to it, such things as
the Beck case and the Slater case are sure to result
even with the best of police and best of courts. On
the other hand, if the police are mistrusted and their
evidence is treated with suspicion, the prosecuting
agencies are divided and even set against each other,

and the efficiency of prosecutions is impaired. A reasonable balance, attained through the guarantees of the bills of rights, seems the most we may expect.

In another respect the administration of justice is much more difficult on the criminal side than on the civil side. One of the hardest problems of all law is how to reconcile the need of rule with the need of discretion. The general security demands administration of justice by rules and forms. More and more the economic order, with its stress on security of acquisitions and security of transactions, calls for rules in great detail. On the other hand, the moral element plays a much more important part when we are dealing with conduct than when we have to do with property and with economic relations. The moral aspects of conduct do not lend themselves to strict rules. If in order to deter others and to satisfy the public demand for vengeance we have to fit the punishment to the crime, in order to achieve other ends of no less importance we must seek to make the penal treatment fit the criminal. From beginning to end of a prosecution we must rely upon the discretion of officials. But in criminal law the dangers involved in discretion are obvious. All discretion is liable to abuse, and the consequences of abuse, affecting the general security on the one side, and life or liberty on the other side, are much more serious than in civil controversies.

Finally, we must take account of the inherent inadequacy of penal methods. Punishment is the staple resource of the criminal law. It relies upon fear as a deterrent, seeking to create a widespread fear of punishment and to bring this fear home to the would-be offender at the crisis of action. But experience in law has confirmed experience in other fields, that fear is never a complete deterrent. The threats addressed to men by the criminal law, even at their best, are too remote to determine human action when passion, desire for revenge, jealousy, fear of disgrace unless a witness is put out of the way, or even cupidity, are exerting an urgent immediate pressure to commit crime. Moreover, threats of drastic punishment are not unlikely to defeat themselves. Juries prove unwilling to subject the concrete offender to the severe penalties which the zeal of the lawmaker lays down for the abstract offender. It has happened also that pressure upon lawmakers has led them to impose penalties upon acts for which juries will not agree to subject men to punishment. One need but look at the anti-cigarette legislation of the fore part of the present century to find instructive examples. Even judges have been known to warp the law in order to prevent convictions where they were not in sympathy with over-severe laws or extreme penalties. Our criminal procedure still suffers from the astuteness of judges in the past to avoid convictions at a time when all felonies were punishable with death. No matter how carefully we draw our criminal codes or how efficiently we administer them, the inherent inadequacy of penal methods, as compared with the sanctions of the civil side of the law, will affect our results.

III

OUR INHERITANCE FROM ENGLAND

History and Law

We may recognize three chief factors in the administration of criminal justice, namely, men, machinery, and environment. Justice is administered by men. These men administer it by means of legal and political institutions. Also they do so in a certain social and political and economic environment. Our understanding of any of these factors will be superficial unless grounded in history. For history has much to tell us as to how the men came to be where and what they are. Also it has much to tell us of how the environment developed and of what is permanent and significant therein. But we must leave these factors to others. The men who administer justice is a matter best to be treated by the student of politics. The environment of the administration of justice is best to be treated by sociologist or economist. I can only claim some degree of competence to treat of the machinery of legal institutions with which judges and magistrates and prosecutors and police carry on their work. Here, too, history has much to tell us.

Turning to the institutions by means of which criminal justice is administered, we may distinguish the machinery of criminal investigation, the machinery of prosecution, the machinery of adjudication, the substantive criminal law, and the machinery of penal treatment. None of these has been made wholly *de novo* for the work which it now has to do. Everywhere each item has a content developed by past experience and handed down traditionally, or inherited, or borrowed and adapted. Moreover, in each case the traditional or inherited or borrowed material has been given shape with reference to the conditions and purposes of some time and place. This is true especially of criminal procedure and the substantive criminal law.

A body of criminal law is not a simple aggregate of rules attaching definite penal consequences to definite prohibited acts or forbidden occurrences. Nor is the application of the rules contained in any given body of criminal law invariably a simple process of determining the facts and matching the ascertained facts to an exact, preëstablished legal pattern. In jurisdictions in which there are common-law offenses, much scope for judicial finding of the law is involved in application of the established principles which determine what is a misdemeanor at common law. It becomes necessary for courts to try new situations by those principles; and when new menaces to the general security are developing rapidly and the nature and degree of menace are matters of debate, courts may have to pass upon the questions without adequate means of informing themselves fully as to the relevant details. Likewise where all crimes are established and defined by statute, interpretation is needful. This does not mean merely ascertaining the will of the lawmaker with respect to something he had in mind and expressly provided for. Often the need of interpretation arises from his not having in mind situations to which nevertheless the law must be applied, and hence failing to make any clear provision for them. In criminal law, the doctrine that penal statutes are to be construed strictly narrows the field of judicial finding of the law. Yet that doctrine has been much relaxed, and even within its relatively circumscribed limits there is often not a little scope for judicial shaping of the authoritative text. Thus we must take account of much besides the enacted rules, even where the most voluminous and detailed penal codes are in force.

As was said in the preceding lecture, the authoritative materials with which courts administer justice are made up of three elements, namely, precepts, a traditional art, and a body of received ideals. The greater part of these materials is traditional, and in that sense it is true that law is "a government of the living by the dead."

Of the precepts which go to make up a body of law, some are traditional and some are deliberately made by a process of conscious lawmaking. Traditional precepts are developed and given shape by judicial experience and by juristic science. We find them in judicial decisions and in law books, in which decisions are analyzed, systematized, and criticized, and their logical consequences worked out with reference to possible questions of the future. They are applied and made available, as the grounds of decision of particular cases, by the traditional technique of the legal profession, developed by English judges and lawyers from the thirteenth century to the nineteenth, and carried round the world, among English-speaking peoples, as part of the common law.

Legislative precepts are seldom made out of whole cloth. Legislation is not a making of something out of nothing. In large part, the legislature puts in authoritative form what has been worked out by judicial experience or juristic science. Moreover, legislature-made precepts have to take their place along with the traditional precepts in the legal system as a whole. Judicial interpretation and juristic exposition must make legislative and traditional precepts into a consistent, logically interdependent body of laws. Otherwise, the relevant precepts could not be known or found or applied with assurance by courts which have thousands or even tens of thousands of cases before them each year. In consequence, interpretation and exposition, carried on by means of the traditional technique, work over and give shape to the legislative precepts with reference to the traditional precepts. The whole background of interpretation and exposition is traditional. Nor can this be avoided. There is no way in which law can escape from the demand for science forced upon it by the complexity of the phenomena of life in civilized society to which it is to be applied.

Thus the most effective part of the law is the traditional element. The significant precepts are chiefly traditional. Even legislative precepts are largely traditional in substance. They are in great part legislative authoritative statements of traditional precepts. Also the technique of developing and applying legal precepts is wholly traditional, and the received ideals, which furnish the background of interpretation and development and application of precepts, are likewise traditional. We shall know very little of the apparatus of administering criminal justice unless we know its history.

Not, indeed, that history may tell us everything. The materials with which men act are not the whole story. We must know the men who act, the materials with which they act, the circumstances under which they act, and the purposes for which they act. But what men do, under whatever circumstances or for whatever purposes, is conditioned in a peculiar way by what they have to work with. In criminal justice today we must work with the criminal law and criminal procedure of nineteenth-century America, and our task is to make of them a suitable criminal law and criminal procedure for twentieth-century America. The nineteenth-century criminal law, however, both substantive and adjective, was itself a historical product. It was made from the materials of English criminal law and procedure of the seventeenth and eighteenth centuries; and those materials were given shape in rural, agricultural, pioneer America in order to meet the conditions of life in such a society.

From a historical standpoint there are five elements in American criminal law. The first is the inherited (or received) seventeenth-century English criminal law and procedure. I say seventeenth-century because American polity began to diverge from the English polity at the opening of the eighteenth century. Often our polity is that of England before 1688. It belongs to Stuart England rather than to modern England. The second element is independent development of criminal law in colonial America. Sometimes the legally ignorant common sense of the colonists brought about improvements in criminal justice. Sometimes also it led to peculiarly American institutions which have left their mark upon our legal system. The third element is Blackstone's Commentaries on the Laws of England. Although this book was first published in 1765, nearly twenty-five hundred copies were in use in America before the Declaration of Independence. One thousand copies of the first English edition were sold in America, and this exceeded the number sold in England. There was an American edition in 1771-1773, and a second American edition in 1779. From the beginning, Blackstone was the foundation of American legal education, and was treated by bench and bar as an authoritative statement of the English law which we had inherited or received. Even Blackstone's occasional errors passed into our law. The fourth element is American building in the nineteenth century upon post-Revolutionary English decisions. Finally, there is American legislation of the legislative reform movement, which begins soon after the Revolution and continues until the Civil War.

We may well begin, therefore, with the materials which were received from England in the formative period of our institutions, and consider next what was done with them so as to make of them the materials with which we must work today.

The Development of English Criminal Law to the Sixteenth Century

Most important among the primitive legal materials which still have a place in our criminal law is the Germanic idea of the truce or peace—the idea that certain places, certain times, certain persons are exempted from private war, and that a wrong done in such a place, at such a time or to such a person, as a breach of the peace or protection or guardianship of the authority responsible for order therein or for protection thereof, is a wrong to that authority as well as to the person injured. In the Anglo-Saxon polity the king was not the only such authority. There was, for example, a peace of the church. Likewise, one in whose house a wrong had been done to another, could claim that there was a wrong to himself also. But with the rise of more definite political organization, the growth of the king's authority, fostered by the church, which taught that the king was the embodiment of law and order, and the breakdown of kin organization, putting the king in place of the kindred as the protector of the wronged, the king's peace came to absorb or supersede all the others. Thus at common law an indictment charges an act against the peace of the king, and with us, by inheritance, it avers a breach of the peace and dignity of the United States or of a state. We are but beginning to be delivered from hard and fast rules as to the jurisdiction of criminal courts which resulted from this bit of history.

"An act," says the Supreme Court of New Jersey, "must be alleged to be an offense against the sovereignty of the government." It adds: "How can an act done in one jurisdiction be an offense against the sovereignty of another?" In the case which brought forth this pronouncement the court had before it a situation in which one man in New York shot another man in New York who was taken to New Jersey and died there. As the New York statute then read, it appeared that there could be no prosecution in New York because the victim did not die within the state. On the other hand, there was a statute in New Jersey authorizing a prosecution in that state "when any person shall be feloniously stricken or poisoned upon the sea or in any place out of the jurisdiction of this state, and shall die of the same stroke or poisoning within the jurisdiction of this state." But the court considered that the legislature could not give the New Jersey courts jurisdiction where the act took place in New York, even if it had effects upon the general security and general morals in New Jersey, and the offender was before the New Jersey tribunal.

Later, a like question came up in North Carolina.

A man in that state fired across the state line and hit
and killed another who was in Tennessee.   The act
was complete in Tennessee.   But the actor was beyond the reach of the Tennessee courts, nor could he
be reached by them through extradition, since he had
never been in Tennessee and hence was not a fugitive
from the justice of that state.   The state which had
him could not try him, while the state which could
try him did not have him and could not get him.

Quite a different conception prevails in the non-
English-speaking world.   There a crime is laid, not
as a breach of the sovereign's peace, but as a breach
of the offender's absolute duty.   Thus in Scotland,
where the practice is founded on the Roman law, the
indictment does not conclude "against the peace and
dignity of the crown," but instead recites that the
accused "ought to be punished with the pains of the
law in order to deter others from committing the like
crimes in all time coming."   The act was what broke
the peace.   Hence our law has gone on the *locus* of
the act as the basis of jurisdiction, not on the social
danger from the man who was at large in the com
munity.   Roman law, on the other hand, went originally on the idea that the impious offender was a
social danger because the gods would be likely to
visit their wrath upon the community which harbored
him.   It was not hard for the countries of Continental Europe to adopt modern theories of jurisdiction
in the courts of the injured state or even of cosmo-
politan justice.   Such theories did not run counter to
settled habits of thinking.   But it has been very hard

for our courts to understand or accept conceptions of jurisdiction on any other theory than the historical territorial theory of the common law.

Administrative and judicial functions are not sharply differentiated in the beginnings as they come to be in the maturity of law. Much in the historical judicial organization arose out of the exigencies of administration. This is true of the lowest as well as the highest judicial officers. In the older polity the sheriff bore rule over the county. But in the twelfth century the king became jealous of his power and, after trying various expedients, found an effective means of controlling the administration of local government in a practice of commissioning conservators of the peace. The system of justices of the peace developed out of this in the fourteenth century. Successive statutes added to the duties of these officials and developed their jurisdiction until at the end of the sixteenth century the form of commission was revised and put as it has remained in England ever since.

As late as the end of the thirteenth century the duty of arresting offenders lay upon the neighborhood. When the hue and cry was raised every one must turn out and join in the chase. This duty of apprehending criminals passed to the justices of the peace. Indeed, it was not until the nineteenth century that the functions of magistrate and of police were clearly differentiated in England. As the justices of the peace were in origin administrative functionaries for the purpose of keeping the peace, the institution retained administrative features but developed as part of the judicial system. Gradually the work of criminal investigation was set off from the judicial functions and it was committed ultimately to a special administrative agency. But at the end of the sixteenth century such specialization was far in the future. Jealousy of administration and of centralized authority in colonial America and later in the pioneer era of rapid setting up of new states, led to development of the judicial side independently of agencies having to do with criminal investigation and keeping of the peace. Thus not only do all English-speaking countries divorce the two, in contrast with the methods which obtain in Continental Europe, but in this country even now, and in England until the last quarter of the nineteenth century, the two agencies of criminal justice are not infrequently out of harmony or even in conflict.

No provision is made in the beginnings of criminal law for any preliminary inquiry. The neighbors dealt offhand with those whom they caught in the act or on fresh pursuit, and for the rest criminals were presented for trial by what we should now call the grand jury, or through the findings of a coroner's inquest. In the middle of the sixteenth century statutes, apparently suggested by the example of the inquisitorial procedure on the Continent, and its general inquiry whether a crime had been committed and if so by whom, provided for examination of accused persons before admitting them to bail, and later for preliminary examination of all prisoners. As we should look at it now, this was partly a police and partly a judicial examination. Only in the nineteenth century did it become definitely judicial in England. This double character of the examination before justices of the peace, as it came to us in colonial times, has had much to do with the unhappy system of police examinations which has grown up extra-legally in the United States. The idea of separation of powers, so much insisted on in the American polity, made it judicial, with all the constitutional safeguards attaching to a judicial proceeding, before the institution of a modern police had developed, and so left a gap which in practice had to be filled outside of the law.

In a primitive polity the king transacts public business in the courtyard of his house. Thus his "court" is the center of administration where the business of government is carried on in all its branches. One of his chief functions was to do justice. He heard complaints in his court or he went about, taking his court (in the acquired sense) with him, and doing justice in person or with the aid of his councilors and advisers. Increasing complexity of political organization and pressure of business presently required him to commit more and more to his ministers or representatives, and courts in the judicial sense became differentiated. In England, in the twelfth century, the practice had grown up of sending itinerant justices about the country with commissions to administer justice as his representatives.

At first they represented the king in many other respects besides his judicial work. All kinds of administrative and governmental work were committed to them. Also the commissions were of no standard type as to jurisdiction. Some were of general scope, some conferred only a limited authority. At the end of the thirteenth century, however, and beginning of the fourteenth, these commissions came to be issued at definite times and their forms had become fixed. The three which have significance for our purposes are the commissions of oyer and terminer, the commissions of jail delivery, and the commissions of assize. The first were addressed to certain of the king's justices and others, authorizing them to inquire into certain crimes committed in certain counties and hear and determine the prosecutions. The second directed the commissioners to deliver the jail of a certain place, and try the prisoners there confined. In time, the first and second were directed to and carried out by the same persons. The third authorized the commissioners to try the assizes (i.e., proceedings to determine questions of possession of land held by free tenure) in a certain county. It gave a limited civil jurisdiction. Later these commissions of assize were made to include the powers appropriate to the other commissions and the powers of the commissioners were extended by statutes. In the middle of the sixteenth century it was enacted that prisoners convicted before a judge on one commission might be sentenced by a judge acting under another.

Thus before the era of colonization, these commissions had developed into courts, and had become a settled part of the common-law judicial organization. Likewise, the judicial work of the justices of the peace had acquired a fixed organization as courts of quarter or general sessions, held for the whole county, with jurisdiction of all crimes but treason (although difficult cases were to be sent to the assizes), from which later times were to differentiate courts of petty sessions, where a certain number of justices had power to impose penalties under the provisions of statutes. In all this we have the beginnings of the régime of multiplication of courts of more or less concurrent and overlapping jurisdiction, subject to ultimate review on the record for error of law, which culminated in the loosely organized, self-obstructing system of nineteenth-century America.

Primitive law does not distinguish between tort and crime. Wrongs are the concern of the injured persons and his kindred except as the resulting private war endangers the peace. But in thirteenth-century England a feeling was growing that crime was something more than a matter which could be adjusted between the wrongdoer and the wronged. The old "appeal" by which the private accuser prosecuted was giving way to the proceeding by indictment prosecuted in the name of the king. For anything short of a serious offense (soon to be called a felony), the victim was remitted to his civil action and could not have an "appeal." Also justices of the peace took over petty criminal justice and "tres-

passes" were in their domain.   Later, this type of
trespass was recognized as a distinct class of crime,
under the name of "misdemeanor."   The civil side
of trespass developed into our modern law of torts,
while for a time the criminal side was dormant.
Hence in the later Middle Ages, the criminal law was
powerless with respect to many serious injuries to
person and property.   In the sixteenth century this
defect was met by statutes and by the growth of the
criminal jurisdiction of the king's council.   Statutes
developed the criminal side of trespass and led to
the differentiation by which the word "trespass"
came to be used only for civil wrongs, and "misdemeanor" became the technical term for wrongs less
than felony which could be the subject of a prosecution.

As to the king's council, it was an administrative
rather than a judicial body.   But the necessities of
good government called upon administration to meet
the deficiency in the law.   Moreover, the administrative and the judicial are not capable of exact separation and the two functions, both originally belonging
to the king, were far from any thoroughgoing differentiation at this period.   Such things as riots,
violent trespasses, conspiracies to injure others, attempts falling short of commission of the intended
crime, interference with the administration of justice,
frauds, and other conduct against good morals or the
general security, called for repression without waiting for legislation.   The king's council had the
needed administrative powers, under the vigorous

rule of the Tudors, and was able to develop a judicial side, representing the king as fountain of justice no less than as *pater patriae*. Thus it could work out what became recognized specific common-law misdemeanors as well as principles which later gave us a general doctrine of common-law offenses. At the time of colonization this development was still in progress. It had gone far enough, however, so that the executive and legislative justice, which had to deal with such matters in the colonies, were not without some guidance from the outset.

Such were the substantive and institutional materials of criminal law, as they stood on the eve of colonization. But something less palpable is yet of no less importance because of its indirect effects. The spirit of the medieval English criminal law must likewise be taken into account. At the end of the sixteenth century, English criminal justice was still in its spirit close to the neighborhood self-help or private quest for vengeance on the part of the victim of wrong or his kindred, out of which it had grown. Likewise, it had grown up with the rise of royal authority at the expense of local, feudal jurisdictions, and had still some way to travel toward setting off the judicial from the administrative. Also it had grown up in a time of turbulence and struggle of organized government to attain the paramount position as an agency of social control, which we now take as a matter of course. Being a substitute for vengeance, it was brutal. For any serious crime the punishment was death. Being a product of the growth of royal authority, its procedure bore heavily upon the person accused in the name of the king, and gave every advantage to the crown. Being administrative in origin and often in spirit, in spite of the fundamentally accusatory, rather than inquisitorial, character which it inherited from Germanic law, all the legalism which the Middle Ages could impose upon its procedure could not do away with its possibilities of arbitrary action. Thus there was much scope for serious abuses. Having taken form in the struggle between politically organized society and its medieval competitors, the kindred, the church, and the landed proprietors, it could be made to bear oppressively upon individuals in the interest of the political machinery. This was the more a source of friction in the time after the Reformation. It was a time of adventure, of colonization, of commercial enterprise, of development of non-conformist religious associations in place of an authoritative organization, of rise of a competitive individualist society in the stead of one relationally constituted. The spirit of a legal machinery devised to put down local jurisdictions and territorial magnates, above the law and a menace to good order, could be inimical to a rising element in society. For this new element held to rationalism rather than authoritarianism. It believed in a right of revolution, as contrasted with a duty of passive obedience. It stood for supremacy of the individual reason, not supremacy of the government. It maintained non-conformity as against adherence to the establishment.

Reaction from the spirit of the criminal law, as it stood on the eve of colonization, and its consequences in seventeenth-century England and colonial America, dictated some of the most characteristic features of American criminal law as it was in the nineteenth century.

English Criminal Law and Procedure in the Time of Coke

It is usual to put "the first year of James I" as the starting point of American law. The common law is commonly declared by legislation or held by judicial decision to be in force as it was at that date. Roughly it fixes the time when permanent colonies begin. But it has even more significance historically as marking the age of Coke. Sir Edward Coke, Attorney-General under Elizabeth and Chief Justice under James I, is the oracle of the common law. His Second Institute, a commentary on Magna Carta and the old statutes, is the classical introduction to our bills of rights, and, indeed, the source of much of their legal content. His Third Institute, treating of Pleas of the Crown, or criminal law, is an authoritative statement of English criminal law as it was at the beginning of our American polity. His Fourth Institute, treating of the Jurisdiction of Courts, is the authoritative statement of the judicial organization from which ours is derived. Moreover, Coke was a leader in the contests between courts and crown which was a determining factor in our legal history.

His conception of the relation of courts to the fundamental law and to legislation became the basis of our constitutional theory. His commentary on Magna Carta was printed by order of the Long Parliament and set forth the legal-political theories which were to become distinctive of American law. Thus the age of Coke gave shape to the materials out of which we were to make our law.

At the top of the system of courts stood the "High Court of Parliament." But from the fourteenth century it had been recognized that for judicial purposes this meant the House of Lords. There judgments of the King's Bench might be reviewed by writ of error "for error apparent on the record." That is, in a criminal cause the formal record was examined to see whether the judgment of conviction was legally warranted by the indictment, and whether the several prescribed steps in an orderly common-law prosecution appeared by the record to have been duly taken. It was not a review of the case, but a review of the record. The question was not whether the accused was guilty or innocent, but whether the rules of the game had been followed in convicting him. The English Court of Criminal Appeal, set up in 1907, definitely departs from this conception of review of criminal proceedings, insisting on the rules of the game so far as essentials go, but going into the actual case rather than the formal record. With us, on the other hand, the conception of review of the record for error of law appearing on its face, which we inherited, has been developed to its logical consequences and has fixed the character of criminal appeals in all our jurisdictions.

Parliament had also jurisdiction over impeachments, and, as part of its complete legislative competence to do anything and hence to adjudge anything as the basis of an enactment, power, by bills of attainder and bills of pains and penalties, to punish for "high crimes and misdemeanors," or anything which Parliament chose so to regard, even without hearing the offender. This type of legislative criminal justice was employed in the colonies and in state legislatures down to the federal Constitution. In England it has not been employed since the abortive bill of pains and penalties brought against Queen Caroline. The Constitution of the United States forbade it both to the federal government and to the states. Legislative granting of new trials by special act was practised in the colonies and after the Revolution. But early in the nineteenth century the provisions for separation of powers, universal in state constitutions, brought it to an end. Yet impeachment remained, and also in many states the general appellate jurisdiction. In New York, the Senate was the ultimate court of review until 1847. Legislative review did not disappear wholly from our polity until after the first half of the century. Its marks are upon our appellate procedure to this day.

As legislative justice was represented by the jurisdiction of Parliament, executive or administrative criminal justice was represented by the jurisdiction of the Court of Star Chamber "before the King and his Council." According to Coke, it dealt with "enormous and exorbitant causes" which other courts might not "condignly punish." It was a supplement to the common-law system on its criminal side, as the court of equity was on its civil side. It could look into things *mala in se* as well as those prohibited by statute. Thus the limits of its powers depended much upon the personal views of those who sat for the time being. Its procedure was summary, by bill (petition) or information, by examination of the accused on interrogatories, by examination of witnesses, and upon confession. In the political and religious struggles of the seventeenth century, it became odious and came to an end. But the tradition of the tribunal as arbitrary, high-handed, and lawless (a tradition not wholly just) has left its mark on our polity in the immunity of accused persons from any legal interrogation, a rooted distrust of all agencies of individualization of penal justice, and a quest for a government of laws and not of men in connections where we must rely on men rather than on laws.

Judicial criminal justice was primarily the province of the court of King's Bench. Three heads of its jurisdiction, as they stand in Coke's Fourth Institute, are significant. It had jurisdiction at first instance of all pleas of the crown, i.e., all criminal causes. Second, it had jurisdiction to review the judgments of inferior tribunals in all criminal cases. Third, it had jurisdiction to correct administrative errors "tending to breach of the peace, or oppression of the subject, or raising of faction, controversy, debate, or any other manner of misgovernment." Hence, if any one were confined, it could by writ of *habeas corpus* inquire into the legality of the confinement. It could by writ of prohibition keep the different tribunals within their jurisdictions, and thus could in an ordinary action at law inquire into the exercise of administrative authority, treating exact conformity to law as essential to the wielding of administrative powers.

From the first of these heads we derived a tendency to set up courts of a mixed jurisdiction, both at first instance and by way of review, which is only just disappearing in some of our older states and obtained in the federal courts till the last decade of the nineteenth century. From the second we derive the judicial review of convictions which has happily supplanted legislative review. But on another side it has given us double appeals, which we have just begun to obviate, and in some states an unhappy type of review on *habeas corpus* of convictions in coördinate tribunals. From the third we derive the polity of judicial supervision of administration which, carried to an extreme in the nineteenth century, for a time led to a condition of legal paralysis of administrative action and later, by way of reaction, gave us a régime of administrative boards and commissions quite out of line with our traditional institutions.

For the rest, there were the assizes, the quarter sessions, and the jurisdiction of magistrates in petty causes, already spoken of, and borough courts exercising criminal jurisdiction by virtue of charters. In the sixteenth century it was usual to make the mayor and some of the aldermen justices of the peace, and the charters often gave authority to hold a court of quarter sessions. In the more important boroughs there might be a salaried recorder, a lawyer, who became in practice the real judge. Thus there was a transition from courts manned by laymen to courts manned by trained judges.

American judicial organization was affected by this type of tribunal in three ways. We took over the idea of laymen administering justice as magistrates in petty causes. In some states we took over the idea of municipal criminal courts in which the mayor and aldermen sat as judges, perhaps with a recorder as a judge also. In many states we took over the system of concurrent jurisdiction in county and municipal tribunals, which only disappeared in New York in the present century and still obtains in some parts of the land.

In general, the judicial organization of the age of Coke was characterized by want of differentiation of legislative, administrative, and judicial power, with no small part of the administration of criminal justice in Parliament and in administrative tribunals; by frequent conferring of jurisdiction of first instance and by way of review on the same tribunals; and by courts of first instance and for petty causes manned by laymen or on which lawyers sat as judges along with laymen. All of these features are to be seen in our American polity down to the present century.

Criminal procedure in the age of Coke was in transition from the medieval to the modern. Much in the way of modernizing it took place after the Restoration. Much more was achieved after the Revolution of 1688. What chiefly affected American criminal procedure was memory of the unfair advantage it gave the crown, as brought out in the prosecutions of Whigs and Dissenters under the Stuarts. Seventeenth-century judges were expected by the king to be active in the prosecutions tried before them and were not unlikely to lose their positions if they did not procure convictions in political cases. The accused could not be represented by counsel, except to present certain points of law, and the forensic manners of the king's judges and king's lawyers were vigorous often to the extent of brutality. Zeal to correct these abuses was strong in the new world, so largely settled by refugees who had had bitter experience of them in the old world. Even in the seventeenth century the colonies were moving to do away with some of the harsher features of a common-law prosecution, to give the widest powers to juries, and to tie down the trial judge. Thus at the outset the development of criminal procedure in America was set definitely in a direction which it kept down to the twentieth century.

As the substantive criminal law at the beginning of the seventeenth century is set forth in Coke's

Third Institute, it is made up of common-law offenses formulated by the courts through the traditional technique of decision applied to the old Germanic and medieval legal materials, of statutory offenses defined by legislation from Edward I to James
I, and of judicial interpretation and development of
that legislation. Coke made no attempt to systema-
tize this material, even to the extent of an alpha-
betical arrangement. In his First Institute he followed Littleton's Tenures, in which the old land law
was given a systematic exposition. In the Third
Institute he did no more than lump the existing materials under each specific offense, taking up each
head, apparently, in the order in which he ran upon
it in his foragings in the books. Such system as there
is in our substantive criminal law begins with Hale, a
generation later.

In Coke's disordered treatise, along with exposi-
tions of murder, burglary, robbery, larceny and
arson, which are authoritative statements of the common law today, one will find such survivals as heresy,
witchcraft, multiplication (i.e., attempts at transmu-
tation of metals), hunting at night, prophesying,
spreading of rumors, and hue and cry, and such incidents of post-reformation religious struggles as re-
ceiving Jesuits and popish recusants, and bringing
in papal bulls. Many diverse social conditions,
diverse political conditions, diverse modes of thought,
diverse conceptions of the general security are represented in this mass of formulated specific offenses.
There are few principles or generalizations such as

made the First Institute available for time to come as a sound basis for our law of property. The materials of the substantive American criminal law had from the beginning an unorganized, unsystematic, discordant character which they have retained ever since. The Puritan, smarting under the religious and political prosecutions of the Stuart reigns, was strengthened in his feeling that it was "a dark and knavish business" when he looked at the contents of the authoritative book. One effect of this condition of the substantive criminal law in our formative era may be seen later when so many of our jurisdictions contemptuously rejected the doctrine of common-law crimes and thus opened the way to the hypertrophy of our statute books.

With respect to penal treatment, the age of Coke was hardly even in transition from the Middle Ages except that, in reaction from the anarchy of the Wars of the Roses, the criminal law had been tightening. The era of Tudors and Stuarts was one of vigorous exercise of royal authority. Benefit of clergy, which, in the case of offenders who could read, had in the last quarter of the fifteenth century made the law as to felonies farcical, was being cut off by a series of statutes. In Coke's time eight, and by the end of the seventeenth century twelve, crimes were excluded from the benefit of clergy, and so were capital by whomsoever committed. In the case of offenders who could not read, all felonies, including manslaughter, and all thefts of more than the value of a shilling were capital.

What this meant is suggested by the estimate, on credible grounds, that there were on the average eight hundred executions a year in the last years of the sixteenth century. Coke bewails this in the Epilogue to the Third Institute, saying :

"What a lamentable case it is to see so many Christian men and women strangled upon that cursed tree of the gallows, in so much as if in a large field a man might see all the Christians that in but one year throughout England come to that untimely and ignominious death, if there were any spark of grace or charity in him, it would make his heart to bleed for pity and compassion."

For high treason the penalty was hanging, drawing, and quartering. In case of a woman, both for high and for petty treason, it was drawing and burning. For misdemeanors the staple penalty was pillory and flogging. For mayhem there was loss of the like part as that of which the victim had been deprived. For petty larceny the ears were cut off. For other offenses there was branding. Fine and imprisonment were growing into use, but the old punishments held their ground. Moreover, all felonies entailed forfeiture of goods and attainder, making it impossible for the felon's heirs to succeed to his property. Already in the seventeenth century the ideas of humanity, which have always gone along with theories of natural law, were making such things revolting. In an unwontedly eloquent passage at the end of the Third Institute, Coke calls for preventive in place of punitive justice, and invokes a blessing

upon him "that layeth the first stone of this building." The exigencies of strong royal government
were taken to call for drastic penal treatment and
brutal prosecution to the end of the seventeenth century. New economic struggles were taken to call for
a continuance of such things throughout the eighteenth century. Moreover, there had been no experience of any other régime. But men's consciences were
increasingly troubled. Such things as the brutal
flogging of Oates made an exceptionally vivid impression. Even in the seventeenth century, the way
was preparing for the attitude toward penal treatment which became characteristic of the nineteenth
century.

It is not possible to speak of the spirit of seventeenth-century criminal justice as one may speak of
the spirit of medieval criminal justice. The problems were more complex. The fundamental ideas
were less simple and less assured. Criminal justice
was in transition. Even in the nadir of the English
judiciary, under Jeffreys and Scroggs, crudities had
disappeared which had existed under the Common-
wealth. One may see a very real advance between
the prosecutions under Elizabeth and those under
James II. But it is not the survivals from the Middle Ages, significant as they are in a general view,
which are most important for our purpose. The
seventeenth century was marked by the growth of
absolute government throughout Europe. The
French monarchy of the old régime, the monarchy
of Louis XIV, was the political model. Public law,

international law, criminal law came to be thought of in terms of personal sovereigns. We still speak and think in that fashion after the last of the Cæsars has fallen. Vigorous central repression of anti-social conduct carried with it vigorous putting down of spontaneous political and religious activity, and this became increasingly irksome in a rising world of individual scientific and intellectual initiative. The relationally organized society of the Middle Ages had broken down. Restrictions born of the needs of such a society were becoming obsolete. The contests between the courts and the crown, with the courts standing for the "immemorial rights of Englishmen," gave rise to a politico-legal conception of a necessary opposition between state and subject, between society and individual, with the common law standing between and protecting the individual. Coke's commentary on Magna Carta is in this vein, and from it in the right line of descent come the legal provisions of our bills of rights, and the whole spirit of their application. This mode of thinking became classical in American law, and has embarrassed effective criminal justice ever since. The development of judicial checks on administration, on criminal investigation, on prosecution, growing out of jealousy of royal power, and the development of mitigating agencies as checks on the brutality of medieval penal treatment, determined the spirit of the criminal law for the next two centuries.

Even more important was the influence of the Puritan Revolution, with its emphasis on the moral worth of the individual human being, its insistence on non-conformity, its faith in the individual conscience, its distrust of all administrative as contrasted with judicial action. Men were to be "with one another not over one another." Political no less than religious associations were to rest on consent—on a "willing covenant of conscious faith." There was to be a government of laws and not of men. This became the spirit of American criminal justice in its formative period, and it governed our thinking in the nineteenth century.

English Criminal Law and Procedure in the Time of Blackstone

Quite as important as the age of Coke, the age of colonization, is the age of Blackstone, the age of independence. Colonial legislation became significant at the beginning of the eighteenth century, and colonial political institutions became settled in accordance with the ideas of Stuart rather than of Hanoverian England. Colonial judicial organization was taking form by the middle of the eighteenth century, and thus our organization of courts has retained characteristics of Stuart England. But the demand for any detailed development of substantive law was not great until the era of expansion following the Revolution. Blackstone's Commentaries, with their readable exposition of the immemorial rights of Englishmen, furnished convenient weapons in the political controversies leading to independence. The vogue thus acquired was confirmed by the need of a usable statement of the common law in the period of legal development at the end of the eighteenth century and thereafter. Blackstone served both as a manual of the received English law and as the basis for the new start, legislative or judicial, which was demanded by the social and economic conditions of the new world.

English criminal procedure was and is unique in that prosecutions are conducted by private persons or by public officers acting theoretically in private capacities and with few powers to differentiate them from private prosecutors. At common law peace officers and private persons are in much the same legal position as to arrests, the peace officer having only somewhat greater immunity in arresting upon suspicion. The duties of peace officers and of private persons after arrest, and the lack of legal authority to interrogate are the same in each case. As Sir James Stephen puts it, at common law a peace officer "may be described as a private person paid to perform as a matter of duty acts which, if so minded, he might have done voluntarily."

At common law, if the victim of a crime, or some one interested, came forward as prosecutor, he had charge of the proceedings, as he might have charge of an ordinary civil action, except that the king's attorney-general might, in his discretion, stay it by *nol. pros.* Even when the king's law officers, or today the director of public prosecutions or the police, take charge of a prosecution, in legal theory their powers are simply those of a private prosecutor.

This peculiarly English system of private prosecution in the name of the king involved unhappy incidents which were pointed out by Sir Matthew Hale in the seventeenth century. But the office of Director of Public Prosecutions was not set up in England till 1879. In the age of Blackstone, the common-law régime was in full force and the law as to arrests, authority of peace officers, and powers of prosecutors, as we received it, was adjusted to and grew up with and out of that régime. One of the first changes which we made was to set up a public prosecuting authority and do away with the system of private prosecutions.

More than one bad feature of American criminal justice of today comes from want of accord between the law in the books and the administration of law in action when an organized police and organized bureau of public prosecution function under a system of legal rules presupposing private arrest and private prosecution.

Criminal procedure, as it stands in Blackstone's Commentaries, is the system with which we are familiar today. The rules as to arrest are the same, although in the nineteenth century the institution of the police, and in the twentieth century automatic pistols and motor vehicles introduced radically new situations of fact. The system of commitment and bail is the same, variously modified in its details by statutory tinkering in the several states. The system of beginning prosecution by coroner's inquest, presentment or indictment, or in certain cases by information is generally the same notwithstanding the radical change introduced by the system of public prosecution. Some jurisdictions have substituted a medical examiner for the inadequate institution of the coroner. Some jurisdictions also have come to the logical result of the system of public prosecutions and done away with grand juries, a proper check on private prosecutions, as a regular and necessary stage in a criminal proceeding. But that reform lags. Arraignment, plea and issue, trial, judgment, review, reprieve, and pardon stand fundamentally as in the fourth book of Blackstone. The changes are due to the legislative reform movement of the nineteenth century, and are almost wholly in the way of cutting off survivals from the Middle Ages, such as hue and cry, distress and outlawry as process upon indictment, the consequences of standing mute when arraigned, pleas of sanctuary and benefit of clergy, trials other than by jury, and attainder with its consequences. Much of this was obsolete in Blackstone's day, but stood in the books till cut off in England also during the legislative activity of the first half of the nineteenth century.

In comparison with Coke's Third Institute, the substantive criminal law in the fourth book of Blackstone is well systematized. There is a good general account of the scope of the criminal law, of the common-law conception of a crime, of the rationale of penal treatment. There are well defined general principles running through the whole subject. The several specific crimes are taken up in a logical sequence and are systematically expounded. True there is still much obsolete matter, or matter on the point of obsolescence, which it remained for the legislative reform movement to clear away. But these things had little or no effect in the United States, where legislation began to cut them off within a decade from the close of the Revolution. Also there is some legislation of the beginnings of industrial struggles in the transition from agricultural to industrial England. But this was not common law with us and was not received. We had to adapt some crimes, as set forth in Blackstone's exposition, to the circumstances of a different social and economic order. We had to work over some of the materials to meet new menaces to the general security. Yet it is noteworthy how long the substantive criminal law, as we received it, was able to stand and do its work well with no more than amendment of details here and there. Down to the present century, our penal codes, except for minor offenses, were almost wholly declaratory. In the fourth book of Blackstone we had the basis for a good development of the substantive criminal law. Had we gone forward on that basis, as we did in the development of the civil side of the law, there would be little of which to complain so far as concerns the body of precepts to be enforced. The reasons of our not doing so belong in another connection.

When we come to penal treatment, the contrast between Blackstone and Coke is much less marked. Drawing and quartering in case of high treason, and burning of women in case of petty treason still stand. The list of felonies without benefit of clergy, punishable in all cases with death, has grown to one hundred and sixty, reducible, it is fair to say, to about seventeen main heads and perhaps a few more than fifty systematically defined offenses. But this is a fearsome number. For the rest, Blackstone enumerates, as the legal punishments of his day, banishment, transportation, imprisonment, forfeiture of property, mutilation, branding, whipping, fines, the pillory, the stocks, and the ducking stool. He is rarely given to condemning anything which he finds in the law of the land. But he is moved here to add, in the spirit of the philosophical humanity of the eighteenth century, that the catalogue he has set forth is "disgusting." We must remember this when we come to consider the attitude of nineteenth-century America toward the whole subject of crime and punishment.

If on the surface the spirit of eighteenth-century criminal justice seems still very much that of Stuart England, when we look at what was stirring beneath the surface we find something very different. The characteristic of seventeenth-century criminal justice which is most significant is vigorous use of the central legal and administrative authority to repress what are conceived to be menaces to the general security. The significant characteristic of eighteenth-century criminal justice is securing of individual liberty against oppressive exercise of administrative authority or operation of the prosecuting machinery. The factors in intensifying this characteristic, decisive for American justice, are the political ideas of 1688, the conceptions of the province of court and jury which grew out of the beginnings of the struggle for reform of parliament, and the rationalist philosophy and theory of a law of nature which controlled the legal thought of the time.

It was not difficult to interpret the triumph of the Whigs in 1688 as a triumph of individual liberty as against arbitrary governmental action. Such was the orthodox interpretation for more than two centuries. It was a triumph of the ideas of non-conformist and political revolutionist; of resistance to authority, of individual interpretation, of supremacy of parliament and courts, not of crown, of reliance on juries, not on royal judges, of autonomy of local governments as against centralized royal control of the boroughs, of emphasis on individual reason rather than on authority, of insistence on the "right of revolution" rather than on the duty of passive obedience.

Of the two logically inconsistent conceptions expounded by Coke, in different connections and with equal emphasis, and between which he could not choose, namely, the omnipotence of parliament and the supremacy of legal limitations as imposed by the common law and declared by the courts, the former prevailed in England, the latter in America. In England centralized government triumphed, though this result was obscured by the downfall of personal royal rule. In the event, there was a king who reigned but did not rule, and a highly centralized legislative ruler with full powers and no legal limitations. The legislative sovereign was what the Stuarts had sought to make the royal sovereign. But the sovereign parliament did not for the moment appeal to men's imagination as did the downfall of the sovereign monarch. The Revolution of 1688 could appear as a triumph of the atomistic as against the unifying forces in English politics. And this view accorded with the needs of a pioneer world. Moreover, Blackstone wrote in the spirit of the time when he was a student rather than of the time in which he taught. He was as little able to choose between unlimited parliamentary sovereignty and legal limitations on all political rule as was Coke. To American lawyers he seemed to reinforce Coke.

With us, a president or governor has remained a Tudor or Stuart king, ruling rather than reigning, ruling with Congress or the legislature, if he can, and in spite of them if he must; but ruling under the law and sharing his power with legislature and courts, likewise limited by law. Thus if the ideas of 1688 included, on the one hand, sovereignty of parliament, on the other hand, they included legal limitations on political authority, checks on administrative action, freedom of local self-government, and individual liberty. In England, the sovereignty of parliament established a centralized legal and administrative régime. In America, there was no such omnicompetent authority and the current ran far in the direction of Germanic *Kleinstatismus*.

Thus in the formative era of American institutions there were extravagant ideas of local independence. Such ideas made concerted military action during the Revolution difficult and sometimes at critical times impossible. They hampered the military operations of the central government in every war down to the twentieth century. They produced something akin to anarchy from the Revolution to the adoption of the federal Constitution. They led to bitter hostility to ratification of the Constitution, and brought about the first eleven amendments after ratification. Their effect upon American criminal justice has been profound. If our criminal justice in its whole spirit, and in the spirit of its administration, seems out of accord with the economic order of today, we must contrast that unified economic order with the régime of forty-eight bodies of local law and a distinct body of federal law, sometimes pulling together, and very often pulling apart. We must contrast the conception of organized, freely directed, efficient action, characteristic of our industrial order, with the system of checks and balances, tying down legislation and administration, the parceling out of political power, the system of constitutionally guaranteed individual rights standing between the offender and the prosecuting activity of the state, the instinct for independent local action and so tendency toward administrative non-coöperation, and the fear of centralization leading to suspicion of elementary responses to the exigencies of the actual economic order—we must contrast with the spirit of the modern industrial order these things which mark the spirit of our political and legal order.

Throughout the seventeenth century the power of juries to render general verdicts was a chief obstacle to the attempts of the crown to use criminal justice for political purposes. When Bushel's case established that jurors could not be punished for contempt in using this power as their own reasons and consciences dictated, the trial jury seemed to stand first among the common-law bulwarks of individual freedom. Later came the prosecutions for libel and sedition which went along with the rising movement for parliamentary reform. Insistence that the jury might draw inferences for itself, and that it was judge of law as well as fact in such prosecutions, became an item in the program of liberalism and reform. At the same time the colonists were putting their trust in the local jury as against royal judges. Thus trial by jury, with great powers confided to the jury, came to be held the first item among our inherited liberties. This frame of mind, which prevailed at and after the Revolution, must not be forgotten when we look into the extravagant reliance on juries in nineteenth-century America.

Nor should we overlook the philosophical ideas of the time when our law began its independent development. It thought itself an "age of reason." It was skeptical of authority. It conceived that laws and institutions could be devised *de novo* by a sheer exercise of reason. It believed that each individual was competent to exercise his own reason with respect to legal institutions and legal precepts; that the authority of law was derived from the free consent of the individual man. It conceived of the state and the law as government from without, not as public service from within. The enduring realities were individual natural rights. The machinery of an ordered society existed only to secure them and they must be jealously guarded at every turn from misapplications of that machinery. Thus the philosophical thinking of the time helped turn the development of our legal institutions toward emphasis on the individual life in contrast to emphasis on the general security.

IV

CRIMINAL JUSTICE IN NINETEENTH-CENTURY AMERICA

The Background of Our Formative Criminal Justice

If American criminal justice has its roots in English criminal justice of the seventeenth century, it becomes distinctively American in the eighteenth century. American judicial organization, the great body of American legal institutions, and what is more important, the American common law, which is the enduring element in the local law of each state, are chiefly the work of the last quarter of the eighteenth century, and the first half of the nineteenth century. Many things here and there in American law go back to colonial institutions and practices. But for most practical purposes our legal history may be said to begin after the Revolution. Colonial legislation begins in some jurisdictions almost at the outset, and Massachusetts had a statute book of no mean proportions in the first half of the seventeenth century. Yet on the whole, colonial lawmaking did not extend much beyond police regulations until the eighteenth century. Until the middle of that century justice was administered by lay magistrates, by soldiers, clergymen, or administrative officers, and by legislative assemblies, rather than by courts in a modern sense. There are no American law reports till the end of the eighteenth century. The last quarter of the eighteenth century and the first quarter of the nineteenth century is the formative period of American law as it stands today; it is the period in which the English legal materials were received and made over by a body of men learned in the law, sitting on the bench, making law in the legislatures, or lecturing and writing as law teachers. Yet not a little of the spirit of our law derives from colonial America. Some of the characteristic features of our procedure grew out of the offhand application of common sense by lay magistrates in colonial times to the scanty stock of English law and English procedure which had come to their notice. The "freedom and inclination to novelty" which characterize our formative era may be seen full blown in the colonies.

Little more than sound common sense was called for by the tasks of ordering a simple society in a sparsely settled pioneer community. Common defense was the first concern. For the adventurous there was the safety valve of the wilderness at every man's back door. There was little need of technical preparation for the work of judging. It was long before practice before the colonial tribunals called for much technical skill or knowledge. Judge Hough, writing of the Court of Admiralty of the Province of New York, as it was in the first quarter of the eighteenth century, says that "neither bar nor bench was doing more than using what they knew of general law, wholly untrammeled by any traditions of admiralty as pursued in England." The practitioners in admiralty were the first specialized bar in America and were very much the best practitioners of the time. Judge Hough says of them: "They were distinctly eminent citizens, they knew very little of historic admiralty, but they were quite capable of devising methods of getting business done, and did it." Less able men in less specialized fields could achieve something by mere common sense and blundering.

We know from the testimony of an English barrister, who practised for a time in seventeenth-century Massachusetts, that the magistrates were impatient of anything beyond a necessary minimum of law. The first American law books are manuals of practice before justices of the peace. The records of the magistrates show that they administered a rough and ready summary justice according to their views of what good order and the general morals called for. Gradually, the economic development of some of the colonies required courts manned by trained judges and assisted by a learned profession. But little of what was decided by American courts before the Revolution was reported or left in a condition to be used in the era of legal growth. Perhaps the chief legacy of the colonial period is the system of petty courts manned by laymen which still obtains except as superseded by municipal courts in our larger cities.

Both in England and in America, the traditional legal materials were made over, partly by legislation

and partly by judicial decision, in the first half of
the nineteenth century. Much of this work of re-
making was done in the course of the legislative reform movement (1776-1873) in which the traditionally received criminal law was pruned of survivals
of medieval brutality. Much more was done by judicial decision, reshaping the received materials to the
conditions of an individualistic economic order in an
era of enterprise and of exploitation of natural resources; an era when men were specially impatient of
regulation and expected the legal order to say "can"
rather than "can't." But there was a significant difference. In England this movement made over the
seventeenth- and eighteenth-century legal materials
to the needs of an increasingly urban and industrial
society. In the United States, we made them over
to the needs of a pioneer, rural, agricultural society.
Thus, when the change from a rural, agricultural to
an urban, industrial society became manifest in
twentieth-century America, it found a well developed
and well established body of legal institutions, legal
precepts, and legal procedure adapted to a wholly
different social and economic order.

What is law in the books is largely determined by
history. What is law in action is chiefly determined
by public opinion. This is especially true in criminal
law. On the civil side of the law there is an aggrieved
party seeking redress and pushing the machinery of
the legal order into action. On the criminal side
there are only the appointed officials, charged with

the duty of setting the machinery of detection and prosecution into action, but too often impelled by any strong sense of that duty only in matters as to which public indignation is strong or public interest keen. Moreover, public opinion has a very real place in the law in connection with the ideal element. The received ideals of the social order, and hence of what the legal order should be, which are decisive of the development, the interpretation, and the application of legal precepts, are directly and immediately influenced by the prevailing opinion of the community as to things that are done and things that are not done. Received ideals, traditionally formulated to the opinion of the past, change their form and their content under the pressure of the opinion of the time. The personal ideals of judges, which govern in matters left to their discretion, will reflect consciously or unconsciously the prevailing views of the time and place as to the ends of the legal order, and hence the purposes of what they are called upon to do. If we are to understand anything of criminal justice in nineteenth-century America beyond its bare doctrinal content, we must look into its ideals as fixed by the opinion of the time in which they were formative.

Four ways of looking at things political and legal left their mark upon nineteenth-century criminal justice. In some sense they are no doubt four phases of one mode of thought, as looked at from different standpoints. But it is convenient to take them up one by one as the pioneer attitude, the natural-rights attitude, the democratic attitude, and the entrepreneur attitude.

All social and political institutions are affected for time to come by the modes of thought and habits of action of those among whom they originate. A community will bear the stamp of its original settlers long after the descendants of the first settlers have passed on. New England still has the mark of the Puritan, New York of the Knickerbocker, Pennsylvania of the Quaker, Virginia of the Cavalier, South Carolina of the Hugucnot, Louisiana of the Frenchman of the old régime, central California of the Spaniard, San Francisco of the 'forty-niner, Kansas of the Free-soiler. For like reason, American legal institutions are characteristically those of the pioneer. Except for a narrow fringe along the Atlantic coast, one has but to scratch the surface anywhere in the United States to come upon the pioneer. Cooper's story, "The Pioneers," describes central New York as it was known to the grandfathers of men now living. The generation which saw the Civil War had grown up in the pioneered country between the Alleghenies and the Mississippi, and those who fought came back to pioneer the prairies between the Mississippi and the Rocky Mountains. Two generations take us back to the discovery of gold in California. The fathers of those still living settled the west, and the pioneers of the Rocky Mountain states are not yet gone. The last state was opened to white settlement in 1890, and admitted to the Union in the present century.

"Some of our worst political abuses," says Professor Sumner, "come from transferring to our now large and crowded cities maxims and usages which were convenient and harmless in backwoods country towns." This is no less true of legal abuses. A rural society in which judicial proceedings were regarded as a spectacle, or a frontier society in which men were prone to set right their own wrongs, conduct feuds, organize vigilance committees, hold lynchings, and exert offhand extra-legal pressure on those whose conduct varied from the locally recognized ethical norm, are in the background of more than one unhappy feature of our criminal justice.

As the pioneer saw himself, his virtues were independence and self-reliance, versatility, a bent for invention and innovation, impatience of pomp and ceremonial, and a preference for short cuts and free and easy methods. But these characteristics are by no means unmixed virtues in the highly organized economic order of today. Self-reliance, impatience of regulations, and faith in one's individual judgment at the crisis of action, are not tolerable in action when displayed by drivers of motor vehicles at crossings of city streets in the face of elaborate systems of signals. Versatility, distrust of specialists, lack of faith in experts, confidence that any man is equal to any task, have had some rude shocks in the present generation. The Spanish-American War is probably the last we shall ever fight with volunteer officers of the type which made Shiloh a classical example. We have found the need of a well trained medical profession, and are finding the need of better trained lawyers. Reaction from belief in innate capacity has since the World War been sending a whole people to institutions of learning. In the domain of politics we are increasingly driven to employ trained experts in the public service. We are not so sure as we were that a vigorous physique and a good conscience are all that is needed for the criminal investigator. Invention and innovation, when applied to political institutions simply by way of satisfaction of individual creative impulses, have ceased to be valued in a sensitive economic order resting upon credit and carrying on long-time enterprises. A certain measure of ceremonial has proved to have value in a more crowded world and more stable society with more complicated tasks. Taylor and Grant are probably the last of American commanders to direct armies in civilian dress, or in the uniform of a private. Our judges now wear robes. We have found that decorum in court tends to the rapid and orderly dispatch of business on the huge calendars of today. We have been learning that forensic dignity and good manners help make justice effective by making it respected. Not a little which is currently denounced as a newborn lawlessness, or as decadence in the moral fibre of the people, is no more than the characteristic virtues of the pioneer past, functioning out of place, or the gropings of the descendants of the pioneers in their efforts to adjust to an urban, mechanical civilization.

More specifically, three features of American pioneer society have had far-reaching effects upon our criminal justice.

A pioneer society was in some sort a Cave of Adullam; "every one that was in debt and every one that was in distress, and every one that was discontented gathered themselves there." Not unnaturally, the Adullamites had an underlying sympathy for the fugitive from justice, or, as they were apt to call him, "the under dog." Mark Twain's story of the petitions to the Governor to pardon Injun Joe illustrates this tendency, for a caricature often brings out characteristic features better than a photograph. As late as 1909, at the National Conference on Criminal Law and Criminology, an experienced prosecutor pointed out that the old-line American, when he sat upon a jury, was predisposed to release the accused—his first thought was "let the fellow go." Moreover, the Adullamites, who had control of the local law and procedure, and were not minded to be pursued into the wilderness, rejoiced in a procedure which was full of pitfalls for prosecutors and of opportunities to divert a cause from the merits to niceties of practice.

Another and no less unfortunate effect of pioneer or frontier opinion upon the criminal justice of the nineteenth century, and hence of today, may be seen in the law as to insanity and the discredit of expert evidence, chiefly in homicide cases but extending from such cases to every branch of the administration of

justice. In a paper read before the American Bar
Association in 1906, entitled "The Jurisprudence of
Lawlessness," Mr. Kernan formulated the so-called
"unwritten law" or "higher law," which represented
the opinion of the last century, or at least of frontier
societies in the last century, as to cases of injury to
domestic relations or family honor, imputations
against female members of a family, and insults to
the dignity of a man sensitive as to his "honor."
In such cases public opinion justified killing, and
until recently juries would not convict. Yet the
decencies frequently required a prosecution, if with
no other result than to afford a public spectacle.
Hence, it was necessary to invoke some fiction of fact
upon which to hang the defense and acquittal. The
defenses which became standard for such cases were
insanity at the time of the killing and, in cases of
shooting of one prominent citizen by another, growing out of alleged insults or violent differences of
opinion, self-defense. In order to get the defense
of insanity before the jury, alienists were called in
as witnesses, and the extravagant theories which they
gravely propounded in such cases, invoked presently
for other cases where the "unwritten law" was inapplicable or less applicable, drove courts and legislatures to warp the law as to insanity and make of it
a logical muddle.

Accepting the starting point of the criminal law
of the last century, namely, that a criminal was a
person possessed of free will who, having before him
a choice between right and wrong, had freely and de-

liberately chosen to go wrong, it was evident that if mental disease inhibited or destroyed the will element or precluded the choice of right and wrong, there was no crime. Upon this simple and intelligible foundation, the ingenuity of alienists, employed as medical advocates in unwritten-law cases, built a plausible superstructure of "irresistible impulse," "emotional insanity," "brain storm," and the like, which, while it deceived no one, made it appear that the law had been satisfied and brought the legal result into accord with public opinion. But these alienist theories came to be used for other cases for which they had not been designed. Also public opinion began to change as to the "unwritten law." With the passing of the frontier the general security came to weigh more, and the so-called "honor" of the individual free man less, in the moral scale. As Mark Twain put it, we perceived we had made a mistake in seeking to punish murder; it was not murder which menaced society, but insanity. We should have made insanity a crime. Accordingly courts and legislatures set out to curb the defense of insanity. Many courts did this by cutting off all consideration of one of the two elements of a crime, as affected by insanity. Some did it by an arbitrary rule as to the burden of proof, departing from the whole underlying theory of the orthodox criminal law. Some legislatures sought to do it by going to the extreme in both of these directions. Thus it happens in some jurisdictions that insanity is dealt with in one fashion in a case of homicide and in another in a case of larceny. No doubt better theories of criminality will presently make these anomalies obsolete along with the general principles to which they are irrational exceptions. Yet they will have done mischief for a long time if only in making the law appear a mass of arbitrary rules.

But the mischief of the old "unwritten law" cases did not stop with confusing the law as to insanity. They brought medical expert evidence—indeed all expert evidence—into thorough discredit and thus hampered the legitimate use of expert evidence in prosecutions for at least a generation after the "unwritten law" had begun to lose its efficacy. We should not forget that it is nothing inherently wrong in the common-law conception of a trial, nor in the common-law practice of expert evidence which has brought discredit upon this branch of our law and practice, but the deliberate abuse by trial lawyers and medical experts, originally with the assent of the public and to meet the demands of public opinion, so as to square the law in the books with the results in action demanded by the ideals of a frontier society. Naturally the abuse outgrew its original purpose, spread to every part of our administration of justice, and makes trouble after its occasion is on the way to be forgotten.

Next to frontier ideas as to justifiable killings, pioneer faith in versatility and distrust of specialists and experts as such have contributed toward the backwardness of our criminal justice in the use of the resources of modern science. Extravagant reliance upon the common sense of juries, tying down the trial judge and preventing any effective participation on his part by commenting upon the testimony of witness-advocates, a faith that the ordinary man can judge offhand of matters which depend on scientific method and knowledge developed by a long succession of research, keep alive in many jurisdictions crude doctrines and practices antedating the achievements of modern science. The evil these things wrought lives after them; the good is gone with the pioneer conditions which gave rise to them.

I have already spoken in another connection of the effect of legal and political theories of natural law and natural rights in fortifying the impatience of restraint which is encountered in any legal ordering of society. But the influence of such theories must be emphasized as an element in the background of criminal justice in nineteenth-century America. The Declaration of Independence had pronounced it a self-evident truth that all men were endowed with certain inalienable rights—rights which could not be bargained away by consenting directly or indirectly to any lawmaking—rights above and beyond the law, which the law existed to protect and from which it could not be suffered to derogate. In the eighteenth century, these rights were regarded as rationally demonstrable qualities of the abstract perfect man. In the nineteenth century, they were taken to be logically deducible from the abstract idea of liberty. In either event, what they were in detail, beyond certain generally admitted fundamentals, depended on the content each thinker or writer put into the abstract perfect man or on what content he put into liberty. It was assumed that there was a standard abstract perfect man, or that the idea of liberty was given to all of us with a fixed content. But the details in either case have always provoked bitter controversy in any clash of interests. In a homogeneous pioneer society these clashes were seldom serious or far-reaching in their consequences. In a diversified industrial society there is and can be no general agreement as to the details of natural rights.

In effect, the political and legal theory of the last two centuries makes each citizen the ultimate judge of whether his natural rights are infringed. If, as he sees it, they have been, then he is justified in refusing to obey the legal precept which goes beyond the permissible limits of lawmaking. He is justified as a juror in rendering verdicts of not guilty when his fellow men are prosecuted for breaking laws which he and they concur in holding violations of their natural rights. The doctrine that jurors were judges of the law belongs with this ultra-individualist political and legal philosophy. The citizen is invited to judge for himself at the crisis of action whether and how far to obey or enforce the law as it stands in the books. As juror he is judge of the law not merely to ascertain what it is, but to judge of its conformity to his personal ideals and to ascertain its validity.

Consequences of this doctrine, which to the last century seemed one of individual assertion of natural liberty against governmental oppression, look very different today. Today law must bear a far heavier burden of detailed adjustment of relations and overlapping claims, involving far more possibilities of individual dissent. Assertions of a super-legal right of private judgment, such as were made habitually by statesmen, publicists, and lawyers of the nineteenth century, are anachronisms. Those with whose ideal of the social order the particular claim backed by private judgment happens to conflict pronounce the exercise of private judgment as to things governed by the law sheer lawlessness. Yet so deep-seated is this mode of thinking that the same conscientious and well-meaning citizens who challenge private judgment in others, insist that even constitutional guarantees, as well as the settled common-law safeguards of accused persons, shall give way to what their private judgment assures them is enforcement of the paramount law.

In the latter part of the nineteenth century, the doctrine of natural rights was given new vigor by the vogue of Spencer's philosophy. Spencer objected even to laws securing the public health at the expense of individual freedom. He conceived it wrong even to compel an owner to clean up his premises in order to safeguard against epidemics. In the era of social legislation, health laws, housing laws, factory acts, pure food laws and the like, this mode of thought was eagerly taken up both by those bred in an atmosphere of pioneer distrust of interference with every one doing as he liked, and by those who feared that the régime of private property would be weakened. Such legislation was regarded by many as arbitrary and without warrant in natural law. Every one felt justified in judging for himself how far to hew to it or how far it should be enforced. Hence it tended to be enforced spasmodically, as from time to time some disaster shocked the public conscience. The ineffectiveness of these laws, which came more and more to touch the most vital interests in an urban society, hastened the advent of administrative justice and the discredit of the criminal law as an enforcing agency, which went with the rise of boards and commissions in the fore part of the present century.

Democratic ideas as well as philosophical theories reinforced the pioneer attitude toward the criminal law. Our polity had its roots in the era of the Puritan Revolution. It was established as an independent polity in the era of the American Revolution. It was formulated in a written constitution in the era of the French Revolution. Thus the whole emphasis is on liberty as contrasted with order, on rights as contrasted with duties, on checks upon government as contrasted with efficient government, on the dangers of governmental oppression as contrasted with the menace of anti-social individual action. On its political side, liberty was formulated in a contract theory of government, and to Jefferson the social contract was a simple contract, rescindable by dissent as well as originating in consent. The binding force of law, which in the Middle Ages had been rested on authority and in the seventeenth century on intrinsic reasonableness, was referred to the consent of the governed. Laws, which in the era of absolute governments in seventeenth- and eighteenth-century Europe had been declarations of the will of the sovereign monarch, were now taken to be declarations of the will of the sovereign people. It was easy to overlook any distinction between collective consent or collective will and individual consent or individual will. Not a little of lawless or downright unlawful neighborhood enforcement of neighborhood ethical custom in nineteenth-century America is based on an assumption that the formality of consent or declaration of will in the constitutionally appointed manner may be dispensed with.

Another source of difficulty in the administration of justice in the last century grew out of conflict of the idea of omnipotence of the popular will with the idea of checks and limitations upon governmental action. From colonial times down at least to the impeachment of Andrew Johnson, the legislative department claimed to be peculiarly the organ of the popular will. In consequence, conflicts between courts and legislatures took the place of the conflicts between courts and crown in Stuart England. Legislative oppression of those politically opposed to the majority in control of the lawmaking machinery was rife after the Revolution and led to constitutional prohibition of bills of attainder, bills of pains and penalties, and *ex post facto* laws. Legislative attempts to relieve economic depression after the Revolution at the expense of creditors, led to constitutional prohibition of state laws impairing the obligation of contracts. But the legislatures claimed to be the judges of the scope of these limitations, and contests between courts and legislative assemblies over legislative high-handedness begin at the outset of our polity. Legislative disregard of the Jay Treaty, legislative disregard of the guaranteed rights of Loyalists, legislative disregard of the guarantees of the constitution by directing summary convictions in order to force a depreciated currency into use, mark the very beginnings of our constitutional law. Even well into the nineteenth century legislatures would often call the judges before them to answer for their refusal to enforce an unconstitutional statute, and would claim authority to interrogate them as to their decisions. In two states, judges were dismissed or legislated out of office in order to assert legislative supremacy. Moreover, under a written constitution political questions were so often legal questions that, as in the Dred Scott case, a judicial decision might seem a political pronouncement and might become the subject of political controversy.

In the event the doctrine of supremacy of the law triumphed over the democratic idea of supremacy of the legislatively declared will of the people. But the effect upon regard for laws of our régime of judicial upsetting of statutes must not be overlooked. The spectacle of continual clash between law-making and law-applying agencies was not conducive to a public feeling of the sanctity of law. In many jurisdictions in the last century statutes were so commonly and easily overthrown by judicial decision that legislation came to be regarded with scant respect. An elective judiciary, short terms, recall of judges, and recall of judicial decisions, are some of the bad results of this long contest.

While the doctrine that the legislature is the direct organ of the popular will, and hence like the popular will legally omnipotent, or that its enactments were beyond question by a merely co-ordinate depart- ment of government, was being urged, it happened that certain masterful federalist judges set them- selves to check the rising tide of Jeffersonian democ- racy. The prosecutions under the Sedition Act were many of them anything but creditable. The im- peachments which followed, when Jefferson's party got the upper hand, are among the least creditable features of our legal history. But the provocation was great and the putting of the courts into politics was a natural consequence. If democracy was to pre- vail, the ultimate authority as to the existence and interpretation of rules of law could not be suffered to be beyond immediate popular control. Here, too, the net effect was to weaken the legal order and strengthen the attitude of the pioneer and of the political philosopher toward rules of law interfering with liberty.

Entrepreneurs stand to our industrial order as the pioneer first settlers did to our agricultural order. Indeed, they best represent the spirit of the pioneer in the society of today. They have been as impatient of legal obstacles to full and free industrial activity as the pioneers were toward traditional precepts of English law which they deemed inapplicable to the geographical or social or political conditions of the new world. Nor was this attitude of the entrepreneur toward the law without reason. The legal materials given shape for a rural, agricultural society were not always well adapted to the newly arising industrial situations which they had to govern. Like the pioneer, too, the leader of industry was independent, self-reliant, versatile, inclined to business innovations demanding legal changes, and given to short cuts to desired results. Laws seemed to him, as to the pioneer, at best a necessary evil. He felt that if a rule of law interfered with a business project, or even only with some detail of one, there was no time for formal repeal or formal amendment. A way round must be found, by resort to the constitution, by interpretation, or if necessary by specious evasion. His frequently expressed contempt for statutes, his demand that they be given, if need be, a spurious interpretation to conform to his purposes, his ability to retain the ablest minds to aid in compassing his desires, confirmed the ideas about legislation which had developed under pioneer conditions. They helped establish the characteristic American attitude of the last century, which we are now beginning to call lawless—the doctrine of permissible private judgment as to obeying laws, the conception of legislative enactments as characteristically arbitrary and unreasonable, and the rooted antipathy toward the inevitable detailed police regulation which must go along with a highly specialized economic order in a crowded urban society.

We deceive ourselves much when we speak as if the founders of our polity and those who came after them for more than one hundred years walked steadfastly in the paths appointed by law, whereas their successors in present-day America are given over to lawlessness. Examples of widespread public and general disregard of laws in colonial times, after the Revolution, and in the nineteenth century are abundant and suggestive. In colonial America the trade acts were unpopular and systematically violated. A foreign observer wrote of New York that "the inhabitants engage in contraband trade with marvellous skill," and the cases in admiralty in the Province of New York published by Judge Hough quite bear out the statement. Resistance to the Stamp Act was not merely passive nor carried out with due regard for law. Those who threw the tea overboard have been held up as examples to generations of young Americans. John Adams's letters bear witness to mob spirit before the Revolution from which lynchings and white-cap floggings and night-riders are in the right line of descent. The economic depression after the Revolution produced Shay's Rebellion, the excise laws of the newly-set-up national government led to the Whisky Insurrection, the demand for revision of a state constitution led to the Dorr War. No lawlessness in the present century has risen to the proportions of rebellion, insurrection, or war. Laws against duelling, involving the most drastic penalties, were repeatedly enacted and systematically ignored until public opinion brought the practice to an end. The first building of convents in New England led to riots and burnings. The Fugitive Slave Laws were broken openly by the most conscientious of citizens and resistance was carried so far that the Supreme Court of one state obstructed their execution notwithstanding the plain mandate of the Constitution. Violent lawlessness during the era of Reconstruction, riots during the struggle for organization of labor, are within the memory of those now living, and ignoring of the Fifteenth Amendment continues to the present. Our tradition of free individual and collective self-assertion in the face of laws which do not appeal to us as reasonable, of things which offend our ideals of what an American society should be, and of grievances which we are moved to urge for immediate action, is long and continuous.

And yet, on the whole, nineteenth-century America was an orderly, law-abiding land. The infringements of law by good citizens which have been cited, the violent assertions of private judgment against statutes, the mob enforcements of the ethical custom of the locality, for the most part had behind them conscientious belief in a body of law of higher authority of which each individual's reason was the repository. As a people we have never believed in government doing for men what they could as well do for themselves. It was entirely possible for men who respected law and believed in order, believing also in natural rights and in sovereignty of the people, to conceive that offhand popular action, in accordance with what their reasons and their consciences dictated was lawful in all but form. It is easy to point out the divergence between nineteenth-century legalism in thought and extra-legalism in practice. It is easy to show the logical inconsistency of insistence upon a government of laws and not of men, upon constitutional guarantees of individual liberty as legal precepts to be enforced in ordinary legal proceedings, and upon the supremacy of law, on the one hand, and the tradition of extra-legal assertions of liberty and popular sovereignty throughout our history, on the other hand. The discordant elements which had come into our legal and political theory made it logically self-contradictory. Yet the polity itself was workable.

It was for such a society that our judicial organization, our prosecuting organization, our substantive criminal law, and our criminal procedure became settled in the fore part of the last century. We must note the conditions of enforcement, the types of crime and the types of criminal which they presuppose.

As to conditions of enforcement they presuppose an old-time American farming community, when such cities as there were would now be thought no more than large country towns. Thus they presuppose a homogeneous population, jealous of its rights, yet zealous to keep order, except as what it feels to be its liberties are abridged or its moral and religious feelings are shocked, and then moving with more or less orderly self-help toward the ends of the legal order by a short cut. They presuppose a population in sympathy with the institutions of a government which it has set up, which it understands, and in which it believes. They presuppose a population which in all ordinary matters will conform to the precepts of the law as ascertained and made known, which may be relied upon to set the machinery of the law in motion of its own initiative when wrong has been done, and to enforce the law steadfastly and intelligently in the jury box. Rural, agricultural America did not wholly realize this ideal, but it did so sufficiently for practical purposes.

As to the criminal, it was assumed that he was a neighbor who had gone wrong for the time and the action in question; that he was one whose character and qualities were known to the jury of the neighborhood who were to try him. Hence the occasional criminal, the criminal of passion, and the mentally defective were the types of offender for which the law and procedure took shape. The task of criminal justice was to restrain such offenders in a homogeneous pioneer or rural community, in a society little diversified economically, and for the most part restrained already by deep religious conviction and strict moral training. Moreover, the wilderness was near at hand to be conquered, or an unsettled domain was accessible to be opened to human use, or natural resources were awaiting exploitation, to absorb the energies of the irrepressible and adventurous. There was no organized professional criminality on a large scale, operating over the whole country, but at most occasional bands of robbers or cattle thieves such as could be dealt with by a sheriff and posse.

As to crime, there was only the rough virile vice of a community living out of doors. Commercialized vice on a large scale, extending its operations over many localities, was unknown. Nor did large cities with a highly diversified, shifting, industrial population, with extreme divergences of economic condition, with rapid and easy communications with other like centers, with a swarm of people moving back and forth daily to and from a business center and crowding a great volume of business into a few hours afford opportunities for specialized professional crime. Relatively crime and criminals presented simple problems and straightforward tasks to lawmaker, prosecutor, judge, and jurist.

The Substantive Law

English statutes before the time of colonization and those English statutes before the Revolution which were received in this country are part of our common law. The common law was made over in the nineteenth century, partly by judicial decision and partly by legislation. On the civil side of the law, judicial decision was the chief agency of adaptation of the received English law to American conditions. On the criminal side the chief agency was legislation. Thus the relation of common law to legislation has a special bearing on our criminal law.

The cleavage between common law and legislation, which runs through every department, is a characteristic feature of our law. The American lawyer must keep in mind two sets of rules, traditional or common law on the one hand, and statutory on the other. In every quest for the law governing any situation his search must be double, on the one hand in the reports and treatises, on the other hand in the statute books. The traditional or common law potentially covers the whole field but is superseded at numerous points by detailed statutory rules, or even by complete statutory provisions for some one subject, or in some particular field. But our traditional doctrine is that statutes give only rules for the cases they cover. For any new situation the starting point of reasoning is not in the statutes but in the common law; in other words, in the older rather than the newer element of our legal materials. In criminal law statutes in form hold the first place. They have come to define all specific crimes except in some states where the doctrine of common-law misdemeanors is still in force; and even there the tendency is toward minute legislative specification of particular misdemeanors. But the statutory definitions are commonly so drawn as to require resort to the common law in order to interpret and apply them. As we say, the statutory provisions are declaratory. Even when not so meant, the tendency is to make them in effect declaratory by assuming that there was no intention to change the traditional law but only to state it in better form.

During the whole of the last half of the nineteenth century legislation was distrusted both by jurists and by practising lawyers, and, as the substantive criminal law is chiefly in the form of statutes, the effect was not good. It was difficult to make improvements in the definition of old crimes because, no matter how carefully they were re-defined, the courts were likely to say the statute meant no more than to declare the preëxisting law and hence keep to the traditional limits. When new crimes had to be defined, the tendency was to refer them to the analogy of some offence known to the common law, and to interpret the new legislation to that model. Thus the relatively narrow limits of seventeenth- and eighteenth-century offenses were likely to be imposed on statutory attempts to deal with nineteenth-century criminality. The criminal law was made narrow and unresponsive to its problems by this mode of treating the only agency of improvement. The civil side of the law could and did grow by judicial decision. But almost at the outset we feared judicial development of the criminal law. The relation of the criminal law to politics, the bad experience of the first colonists with common-law misdemeanors as defined for political and religious dissenters, the over-zealous conduct of federalist judges during the rise of Jefferson's party led to a settled requirement of legislation for the definition of crimes and development of punitive justice. Yet legislation was hampered by the doctrine that it was presumably declaratory, and by the disinclination of courts and lawyers to give to penal statutes any wider application than the letter required. It was a common-law maxim of statutory interpretation that penal statutes were to be strictly construed.

Partly this attitude toward statutes is an item of the common-law tradition. Partly it is a result of the doctrine of the historical jurists, who were dominant in the science of law in the last century. Those jurists were under the influence of reaction from the sanguine lawmaking of the era of the French Revolution. They insisted on the continuity of institutions and traditions and doctrines as against Jefferson's contention that all constitutions and laws lost their binding force after nineteen years, and hence that legal and political institutions should be made over every twenty years, as it were out of whole cloth. The classical political economy, with its emphasis on leaving men free to assert their natural powers in competitive achievement, the disinclination of the pioneer toward even the necessary minimum of supervision or regulation, the insistence on individual liberty in our political tradition, and later the positivist doctrine that we could only observe the orbit of social development but could not affect it by any deliberate or conscious effort, made the teaching of the historical jurists most acceptable in this country. It took root with us much more deeply than in England and persisted longer. As a result, it became "scientific" to deprecate the only effective agency of improving the substantive criminal law, and to expect the law to improve itself, without deliberate or intelligent effort on the part of anybody, by the sheer inherent power of the idea of justice or the idea of liberty.

While the jurists expected the law to improve itself, the practitioners were not troubling themselves about any possible need of improvement. After the creative activity of the formative era had spent itself, the practitioners confined themselves to working out the details of local procedure and of construction of local statutes conceived of as a body of precepts established by local authority and unrelated to any general law. The ensuing cult of local law was in·evitable in an apprentice-trained profession. It was a time of circuit bars and country lawyers. In each state many local county seats were important legal centers instead of, as today, one metropolitan center. The great bulk of the profession was trained in law offices by the apprentice method inherited from the lower branch of the profession in England.

Our first law schools were but glorified law offices, and for a great part of the last century the teachers, even in university law schools, were judges, retired or active, and active practitioners, teaching in the spirit of the apprentice training. Improvement of the law was no concern of theirs. Practice of the law was a species of handicraft. Procedure was a body of rules of thumb for taking a cause through or impeding its progress in the courts. The substantive law was a body of precepts enacted by the local legislature and interpreted by the local courts. The common law, beyond generalities in the text books, was in the local reports. Local anomalies were emphasized in instruction as significant facts of the legal world. Indeed this mode of training led to an exaltation of local law. Legal provincialisms came to be points of pride. That the law of a particular jurisdiction was different in some respect from that of the rest of the English-speaking world, was not something to look into in order to find the reason and discover a possible defect. It was a visible token of the sovereignty of the people of that jurisdiction living under their own law. Thus, while the country was in process of economic unification, it was increasingly provincial in its law. Attempts to improve the criminal law were met not merely with indifference; they encountered positive resistance from lawyers convinced that the local law and practice, as they had learned them, were a precious local possession. Country lawyers, whose influence is preponderant in the legislatures, still maintain this attitude.

Two generations ago the leading university law schools began to cast off the last remnants of the old apprentice training. Creative writing in our law schools, breaking down provincialism and making for a better body of substantive law, begins with Story one hundred years ago, and has gone forward ever since. But no treatises on criminal law have come from American law schools to compare with the writings on commercial law, on constitutional law, on property, on equity, on obligations, on wrongs, and on evidence, which have given stable direction to every important branch of civil litigation. Criminal law is substantially the only branch of American law which has not been affected powerfully and affected for the better by some text book written by a great teacher of law and embodying the results of his teaching and of his study in preparation for teaching. The standard work on criminal law in the United States is still Bishop. It is the only nineteenth-century book which has conspicuously influenced our criminal law. Now in its ninth edition (1925), it still speaks essentially from the date of its first edition (1856). Good as this book was for its time, it is not to be compared, as an instrument for improving the law, with the writings on the civil side of the law, coming from law schools, in which critical scrutiny of doctrinal points and of interrelations of rules and principles had been compelled through the pressure of questioning by students. In effect, students frequently drive their teachers to write better than they know. But our criminal law has not had the benefit of this process.

In their neglect of criminal law, our law schools have only reflected the demands of students and the attitude of the profession. The rise of commercial law, of the law of public utilities, of conflict of laws, the conspicuous rôle played by constitutional law in our public life, and the development of administrative law have challenged the best powers of the teachers because they appealed most strongly to students and led to the best things in the profession. But the result, excellent for the civil side of law, and for public law, has been bad for criminal justice.

While notable strides have been made in the last generation in other fields of the legal order, the criminal law has been relatively stagnant.

The Machinery of Criminal Justice

Any machinery of criminal justice must rest on an effective administrative system of keeping the peace and of criminal investigation. We began with a medieval régime of local sheriffs, coroners, and constables, inherited from England and adapted by us to rural conditions. In the towns there were watchmen or night watchmen, often with a duty of all citizens taking their turn at the watch; an institution going back to the medieval walled town. Usually there was a town or village or city marshal, a constable with no civil functions and some further powers and duties. He was to keep order and did an occasional bit of detection in the event of a sensational crime; but went out of office with every political change. When the rise of cities called for more than the old-time constables and night watch, there was for a time a system of day watchmen and night watchmen, with inevitable friction between them. Very generally the watch was organized by wards or precincts. A police force as we now know it, both in England and the United States, is an institution of the nineteenth century; and in the United States an institution of the latter half of that century. Criminal investigation also developed in the nineteenth century. Indeed, it had its beginnings in nineteenth-century France and was not organized on any effective plan in England down to the last third of the century. Except for a few large cities, the demand for any modern organization was not pressing in America till well past the middle of the century. In consequence our police organization and administration have been affected for the worse by ideas which became fixed before the days of metropolitan centers and industrial communities. For example, the old ward or precinct system was still governing police organization in more than one large city in the third decade of the present century.

On every side the American administrative régime of the nineteenth century was marked by lack of organization, decentralized responsibility, disinclination of officials of coördinate power to coöperate, and abundant opportunities for obstruction in comparison with means for effective achievement of results. Each official was answerable to the electorate and only to the electorate. He coöperated with other officials or declined to coöperate with them, or even thwarted them, as his fancy or the exigencies of politics dictated. Each county had a sheriff and coroner, as like as not acting independently in the quest for publicity in a sensational case, and not infrequently at cross purposes with the independent village or town authorities. Each city had a marshal or his equivalent, each town or precinct or ward its constable, acting on his own judgment and responsible to no superior. The execution or non-execution of laws was a local affair.

In part, this system, or rather lack of system, and consequent hampering of administration, were part of the régime of checks and balances. As Bryce put it, our polity was the work of men who believed in original sin and were unwilling to leave open any door for the potentially sinful official which they could possibly close. In part, it was due to pioneer jealousy of administration. Largely it was inherited from the medieval local organization in England, not wholly modernized even by the time of the Revolution. But we must note that it was not ill adapted to the society of economically self-sufficient rural neighborhoods for which it took form. It begins to break down with the rise of large cities in the second half of the century and becomes intolerable in the urban society of the present.

As to the conduct of prosecutions, we departed radically from the English system by setting up public prosecutors. In the very spirit of our formative era we provided an independent public prosecutor for each local circuit or district, or sometimes for each county. The usual model was the federal district attorney of the Judiciary Act of 1789, suggested partly by the French *procureur du roi* of the old régime, but also made to the pattern of the English attorney-general. He was not made part of any organized administrative system. His powers were those of an attorney-general, and usually he had complete independence as the local organ of the state in criminal matters. Universally, except in the federal polity, he came to be elected, and the federal district attorneys were deep in politics after Jackson. From the beginning, the United States District Attorney was subject to a certain control through the federal department of justice. This was not always exercised in the interests of efficiency; and even today removal by the President is about the only means of compelling a local district attorney's office to do what the central government conceives to be required for a due administration of justice. In the states, except for certain powers of the attorney-general, greater in some jurisdictions, shadowy or ineffective in others, there was no control beyond public opinion and frequent elections. Usually local prosecutor and attorney-general might coöperate or ignore each other or clash as politics or their ambitions dictated. The public prosecutor was conspicuously adapted to the country of independent neighborhoods, with local institutions, local offenders, and problems of local order and security which obtained in the fore part of the nineteenth century.

American judicial organization, as it became fixed between the Revolution and the Civil War, had for its guiding idea to bring justice to every man's back door in a time of independent neighborhoods, sparsely settled rural communities, slow communications, and expensive travel. The model, the English judicial organization of the eighteenth century, was archaic. In the last quarter of the nineteenth century, England made it over to the needs of an industrial era. We took it up at the end of the eighteenth century and made it over to the needs of an agricultural society in a land of magnificent distances. At that time a unified system would have entailed intolerable expense upon litigants and would have aroused insuperable jealousies. As everywhere else, we carried decentralization to the limit and have gone on in the direction of creating more courts and adding more judges ever since.

Today conditions of travel are very different. One may go across the continent in less time and with less trouble than it took to go from some corner of a state to the state capital when our institutions were taking form. There was no need of strong peace magistrates, well organized, with ample facilities, as in the great city of today. There was no need of a single court of general criminal jurisdiction in which the steps in a prosecution could be reduced to a minimum. There was no need of courts continually in session. All these needs were far in the future and did not affect the system which developed in the last century. Three needs determined that system—the need of obviating long and expensive travel on the part of parties and witnesses, the need of developing the substantive law by the decisions of courts on appeals, and the needs of checks upon lay judges, with no special knowledge of the law, and partisan judges using their powers for political ends after the manner of the judges of Stuart England.

English criminal procedure, as we inherited it, made no provision for review of convictions otherwise than by reversal of a judgment for error on the face of the formal record. There was no such thing as a new trial of a criminal case. But the practice of review of administrative convictions before colonial legislatures and the granting of new trials by colonial legislatures after judgment, made us familiar with review of criminal proceedings and granting of new trials for errors of law. Unfortunately review of criminal trials could be made a means of judicial development of the substantive law. For a century this purpose, rather than speedy disposition of criminal causes on their merits, governed our courts, both in their organization and in their operation. In each state they had to interpret a rapidly growing statute book and adjust its multiplicity of penal provisions to the principles of the common law. Hence the chief energies of the courts were taken up with working out for each state a consistent, logical, minutely precise body of precedents. The task of providing rules was before their eyes to the exclusion of the task of dealing adequately with concrete causes. Our nineteenth-century system was not one for speedy disposition of criminal prosecutions and determination of criminal appeals on their merits. It was one for the careful sifting out of the problems of law involved and construction of a body of substantive law through judicial decision.

Our model for the judge was not the independent English judge of the period after 1688, it was the judge of Stuart England, holding at pleasure of the crown, going back to practice at the bar after holding judicial office, and subject to be pulled this way and that in the political contests of the time. The

politics-ridden, often tyrannical, judges of Charles
II and James II, the magistrates and legislators of
colonial America, not learned in the law and administering a crude executive or legislative justice without law, some arbitrary royal judges of the time just
before the Revolution, and the masterful federalist
judges of the rise of Jeffersonian democracy made a
deep impression upon our forbears. Fear or distrust
of these types of judge brought about curtailings of
judicial power to control the trial and hold the jury
to its duty, and had much to do with the practice of
entrusting excessive powers to juries. These checks
were carried still further during the hostility to
courts and lawyers and English institutions following the Revolution and the War of 1812. They were
quite in accord with pioneer faith in versatility and
distrust of specialists. They were carried out to
their furthest bounds and in great detail on the
frontier. In the hands of habitual defenders in the
criminal courts, who had become a well-differentiated
group in our cities at the end of the last century,
they became effective means of defeating prosecutions.

After 1850 the judges in most states were made
elective, often for short terms. Partly the movement
which brought about an elective bench was due to
enthusiasm for a theoretically complete régime of
democracy. All other officials were elective; why not
the judges? Partly it was due to the tradition as to
trial judges which had come down from the colonies.
Not a little it was due to the obstinacy with which

some strong judges adhered to English doctrines and rules and practices, simply as such, and popular impatience of the formal, involved common-law procedure of the eighteenth century, to which so many judges seemed wedded. So far as the criminal law was concerned, the result was still more to enfeeble its administration. Judges elected for short terms lost control over trials. Counsel rather than judges became the dominant force in the courtroom. Elective judges could ill afford to antagonize and took refuge in a purely passive attitude. As they could not insist upon expedition or upon high ethical standards of forensic conduct, without imperiling their positions, unnecessary continuances and postponements, difficulties in obtaining juries, wranglings of counsel, and ill-treatment of witnesses became discreditably characteristic of American criminal trials. It is significant that these things are relatively unknown in jurisdictions in which judicial tenure is permanent and secure.

But here again the system which grew up in nineteenth-century America was by no means ill-adapted to a rural, agricultural society. On the whole, it still works well enough in communities of the nineteenth-century pattern. It is in the urban industrial centers that it has become an intolerable anachronism.

In eighteenth-century England, as in England today, the legal profession was organized in two branches. The higher branch, the counselors or barristers, had the advocate's function. It was their task to appear in court and assist tribunals in the administration of justice. They were centralized at Westminster and organized in societies of immemorial antiquity, which had control of admission, training, and discipline of their members, subject to a certain supervising power of the bench. The lower branch, the attorneys or solicitors, had the agent's function. They represented their clients in their legal affairs generally or in particular cases. They gave advice, attended to searches of titles and conveyancing, managed trusts, and did what has been called "client-caretaking," getting the opinion of a counselor in cases of difficulty. Also they prepared cases for trial and had general charge of the litigation out of court. They were not centrally organized till the nineteenth century, were localized in their practice, and were simply borne on the roll of the particular court or courts which had licensed them. A like differentiation of the advocate's from the agent's function obtains in Continental Europe.

Attempts at differentiation of the profession were made in some of the colonies and persisted for a time, e.g., in New Jersey. But substantially from the beginning it became the settled American practice to maintain no distinction between the functions of the lawyer. The American lawyer is "attorney and counselor at law." He is legally competent to do anything involved in either branch of professional activity. No one who reads English and American trials attentively can doubt that, whatever the good features of the American system, it has had much to do with the unfortunate features of our criminal trials which became established in the nineteenth century.

Many things contributed to our departure from the English model. One was the prevailing distrust of English institutions after the Revolution. Another was the distrust of law and lawyers in the period of economic depression which followed independence. Another was pioneer distrust of specialists and belief that any man was equal to and should be free to follow any calling. Some states threw the practice of the law open to non-lawyers. Some provided that any one might enter the profession with no other qualification than good character. All of them made entrance to the profession easy with a minimum of qualification.

In this merged profession of law the lower rather than the higher branch of the English profession was taken as the model. Lawyers served an apprenticeship in the office of a practitioner. Later, when law schools arose, they were conducted by practising lawyers in the spirit and largely by the methods of the apprentice training. All of this presupposed a handicraft rather than a science of law; and the democratic spirit of the time was unwilling to concede that one handicraft should be distinguished from another or that more should be demanded of a would-be lawyer or physician than of a would-be carpenter or machinist. The economic and geographical conditions which decentralized the courts led to a system of local bars, a distinct local bar for each local court, with no more than nominal organization, and subjected more and more to deprofessionalizing influences, which the professional tradition inherited from England, could only feebly counteract.

For a time the institution of a circuit bar, going about with the circuit judge from one county seat to another, and in constant contact in court and during term time, had a good effect in maintaining standards of things that were not done and keeping alive the professional tradition. But with the rise of cities and the increasing importance of "client-caretaking" and conditions of modern travel, the circuit bar substantially disappeared in the latter part of the century. The lack of centralization, lack of organization, and deprofessionalization reached their height in the last quarter of the century. By that time, a new differentiation into habitual client-caretakers, habitual plaintiff's lawyers, and habitual defendant's lawyers, had grown up, and, in the criminal courts, a group of habitual practitioners in criminal causes. The effect on our criminal justice was unfortunate in every way. Discipline by the courts was invoked only in rare and extreme cases. Effective discipline by bar associations was in the future. All sorts of loose or bad practices came to obtain in criminal causes in large cities, with no real check upon them. Economic conditions turned the leaders of the bar more and more away from the courts and almost wholly away from the criminal courts. Neither the judges nor professional opinion had longer much controlling influence. By the end of the century habitual practice in criminal cases had become the business of a type of politician lawyer, of little standing at the bar, or of the lowest stratum of the profession. When we remember that the Anglo-American contentious procedure presupposes counsel as aids to the court, this turning of practice in criminal causes to unorganized, undisciplined, deprofessionalized, individual moneymakers must be recognized as not the least factor in the conditions of which we complain today.

Penal treatment in the United States, as it became systematized in our formative era, was the result of a grafting of the rationalist and humane conceptions of eighteenth-century natural law, and later the social utilitarianism of the latter half of the nineteenth century upon an inherited system which went on radically different lines. At the end of the eighteenth century our legislation provided for imprisonment instead of death in case of all but one or two felonies. We worked out a prison system independently, parallel with England. We developed the idea of reformatory institutions and of penal treatment directed toward restoration of the offender to useful citizenship. But these new things were devised and given shape for the rural society of the last century. For the rest, there was the jail system, taken over from England, which did not work badly on the whole in the small country county seat, but became intolerable in the large cities and under the different conditions of a later time. The significant point is that our organization of penal treatment began with independent experiments, was grafted on a bad system, and had relatively little time to develop before it was confronted by wholly new tasks. It did not begin to be studied scientifically till the last third of the century. Before it was much more than worked out for rural, agricultural America, we were having to apply it as well as we might to the predominantly urban, industrial America of the present century. At the end of but little more than one hundred years it was in the same need of radical overhauling as was the traditional medieval penal treatment in the beginning of our polity.

Criminal Procedure in the Nineteenth Century

Obvious anachronisms in the details of our criminal procedure, its cumbersome, dilatory, needlessly technical character as a whole, and the excessive number of safeguards, loopholes, and mitigating agencies by which its effectiveness was impaired, attracted attention as soon as the public began to feel the need of improving the administration of justice. Other features of American criminal justice, which enter quite as much into the result, are less apparent on the surface and have attracted less attention. It should be emphasized that reform of criminal procedure is but one item, and not the most important item, in an adequate program of making our criminal justice equal to its tasks. But there is much to be done here. The elements which made the substantive criminal law what it was in the last century were quite as active in criminal procedure and with like results. Moreover, pioneer and democratic ideas of jurors as sole and self-guided arbiters, historical jealousy of trial judges, traditional common-law limitations upon royal enforcing agencies, American political ideas of liberty, and the humane tendencies of the eighteenth and nineteenth centuries were brought to bear with concurrent weight upon our criminal procedure while it was malleable and gave it a fixed form which persists beyond those conditions or their reasons or occasions.

Three characteristic features of American criminal procedure, as developed in the last century, call for notice.

Most significant is the hypertrophy of procedure. This is characteristic of every department of American law in the last century, and, indeed, was true of English law in the first half of the century. With us an extreme of record-worship grew up and persisted —an excessive regard for the formal record at the expense of the case, a strict scrutiny of that record for "errors of law" at the expense of scrutiny of the case to insure the consonance of the result to the demands of the substantive law. This was carried to an absurdity in some jurisdictions, as in the well known cases in which written verdicts of "guily," or of murder in the "fist" degree were held insufficient foundation for a conviction, or in which a conviction of a major felony was reversed because the formal conclusion of the indictment omitted the word "the" in the constitutionally prescribed formula, or the attitude described by Mr. Justice Holmes—the requirement that an indictment expressly negative "every misinterpretation capable of occurring to an intelligence fired with zeal to pervert." Such things are caricatures, but suggestive caricatures, of a decisive feature of criminal procedure in the last century.

Along with this minute scrutiny of the formal record went rigid enforcement of the rules of evidence for their own sake, without regard to their purposes, so that, for example, new trials were granted for violation of rules meant to save the time of the courts, and rigid scrutiny of the charge of the court with respect to its exact accord with the theoretical requirements of an accurate exposition of the law. As it has been put, the requests of counsel for instructions to be given to the jury became in effect an examination of the judge upon the law applicable to the case, in which he must make no mistake on penalty of vitiating the result of the trial. Thus, especially in the last quarter of the century, there was a lavish granting of new trials which had become a distinct abuse. They had come to be granted in about twenty-nine per cent. of the cases reviewed in the federal courts, and in about forty per cent. of the cases reviewed in the state courts. Such things could not but give to the public at large a wholly wrong conception of the purpose and end of law. They gave impetus to what has been called the American "race to beat the law." If the administration of justice was a mere game, neither the players who took part in it nor the public who witnessed it could be expected to yield to the spirit of the law when their interests were served by evading it.

This "sporting theory of justice," as Dean Wigmore aptly termed it, which inquired only whether all the rules of the game had been carried out strictly, and, if any material infraction was discovered, awarded new trials or reversed judgments just as the football rules put back an offending team five or ten or fifteen yards, helped to develop another unhappy characteristic, namely, the tendency to make a criminal trial a spectacle. In its origin this tendency was in part a response to the exigencies of rural life. In the "Mill on the Floss" we have a picture of how litigation could be a relief from the monotony of rural existence. Before the days of the automobile, the movie, and the radio, before urban amusements were available to every farmer every day, along with politics, the criminal trials at the court house were the staple diversion. During "court week" the wagons of the farmers were tied up about the court house square and an appreciative audience watched the fine points of the trial-game as an urban audience might watch the fine points of a professional baseball game. Later this feature of criminal trials was developed further by the press. American newspaper accounts of trials give a bad impression of criminal justice in action beyond the actual situation. They emphasize the wranglings, the abuse of witnesses, the spectacular features at the expense of the evidence and the merits of the case, and this exaggeration of the spectacular features has tended to aggravate them because of the value of publicity to the actors in the spectacle. The effect of such things on respect for law goes without saying.

Finally, the checks and mitigating agencies, which had grown up in criminal procedure for historical reasons already explained, were largely diverted from their original purposes and became so many counters in the game of justice. They were carried out to their extreme logical possibilities by the ingenuity of habitual defenders, and the resulting mass of procedural detail was congenial to our nineteenth-century law, which thought habitually in terms of procedure and hewed zealously to the conception of a "fair trial" as one in which there had been no departure from the rules. An element in the bar arose which was expert in using this mass of procedural detail and in taking advantage of the checks and mitigating agencies to defeat the ends of the law.

Even when these tendencies were at their height, as in many rural communities today, the criminal dockets were not overgrown, and it was possible for a diligent and well informed prosecutor to make the prosecuting machinery work reasonably well by taking infinite pains. But with the rise of great urban centers, with swollen calendars, even in the last century, the burden was becoming unbearable.

The Beginnings of a New Era

A new era in our criminal justice was beginning before 1900, and the movement for better things has been increasingly strong in the past three decades. The hypertrophy of procedure reached its high point about 1875 and began to show signs of abating about 1890. By 1910 it was distinctly on the wane. Today the greater number of courts have given over record worship and are not inclined to insist upon exact adherence to the rules of the game at the expense of vindication of the substantive law. In the present century the attitude of courts toward legislation has improved. For example, they no longer read a necessity for a "guilty mind" into all penal legislation. They do not insist rigidly on strict construction of penal statutes. In most parts of the country the cult of local law is moribund. New and increasing attention to criminal law is manifest in our university law schools. There is a better judicial attitude toward administration. All these things speak of a new spirit, which some day, very likely, will be identifiable as the spirit of the twentieth-century law.

It is a great mistake to assume, as many writers and speakers do, that the nineteenth-century criminal justice in all its details is in operation in every part of the United States today. Yet it is true in the main that we are working with that system, as after the Revolution we had to work with the system of seventeenth- and eighteenth-century England, for our starting point. We can no more keep to the details or the spirit or even many of the institutions of the one than the founders of our polity could keep to the details or spirit or many of the institutions of the other. The agencies of improvement are at work, and have been at work beneath the surface, for a generation. In many respects we had been moving toward better things when public attention was no more than beginning to be drawn to the abuses which are now so generally perceived.

V

CRIMINAL JUSTICE TODAY

The Background of Twentieth-century Criminal Justice

Before undertaking any consideration of the administration of criminal justice in America today, it has been necessary to look into the problems of administration of justice in a homogeneous, pioneer, primarily agricultural community of the fore part of the nineteenth century, and the way in which those problems were met with the legal institutions and legal doctrines inherited from England. We are now prepared to turn to the problems of administration of criminal justice in a heterogeneous, urban, industrial community, and the difficulties in meeting those problems with the legal and judicial machinery inherited or received from England, as given new and fixed shape for nineteenth-century America. First among these problems are those raised by the wholly, and for many parts of the land suddenly, changed background of the legal order.

Something of this has been spoken of in another connection. Enfeeblement of domestic discipline, of neighborhood public opinion, and of the discipline of religious organizations, under modern urban conditions, has thrown an added and heavy burden upon criminal justice.

But it is not merely that household, neighborhood opinion, and religious organization are not the effective restraining agencies which they were in the last century. It is a commonplace that our political institutions are legal and our legal institutions political. Law is an institution of politically organized society. Anything which profoundly affects our political institutions cannot but affect our legal institutions. Primarily our legal institutions are state political institutions. Except for a jealously limited number of subjects of federal concern, our laws are state laws. In the beginnings of our polity the neighborhood, and the state as a wider neighborhood, were economic entities, or corresponded sufficiently to economic entities so that one's economic interest and political relations substantially coincided. Today one's economic life may be in one state and his political situs in another. His economic interests may be in a community widely distant from that of his citizenship. For as a historical remnant from a feudal society, kept alive by the conditions of an agricultural society, participation in politics follows residence, not occupation or economic concern. One's economic existence may depend on legislation or administration in a jurisdiction in whose political affairs he has no voice, while politics at the situs of his residence and citizenship may be powerless to affect his vital concerns. Apart from the rise of diversions to take the place of politics as the farmer's recreation, this change of economic conditions, doing away with the essential relation between local political institutions and administration, on the one hand, and economic interests, on the other, has made for indifference toward politics and especially toward local politics, with which our administration of justice is intimately connected. Nineteenth-century political and legal institutions presuppose continual and intelligent individual participation in politics, and willing and intelligent individual participation in the administration of justice, which we may not expect reasonably in the society of today.

Another effect of new economic conditions is quite as important. The generation which has seen the development of electric light and power, of the gas engine, of the automobile, of aerial navigation, of the phonograph, of the moving picture, of wireless and of the radio, has grown up and lives amid great increase in the resources available for human wants, and corresponding development of those wants. For ability to use the increased resources has developed with the increased resources. Increased production and consumption have made things everyday necessities which were rare luxuries a generation ago. The monotony of highly specialized work has been offset by a bewildering multiplicity of diversions, demanded by all as of course. All these things have made for increased individual self-assertion, which the last century taught us was the end to be promoted by the legal order, and are making for conscious and aggressive individual self-assertion at a time when the general security demands that we think more of an ordered society and of common ends and less of individual freedom to do in all things as one likes.

Even more, the amount and variety of impact upon the individual, as compared with the relatively simple social order of agricultural America of the last century, multiply the problems of conduct, confuse individual judgments as to standards of conduct and their application, and deprive laws of what the philosophical jurists of the past took to be their chief guarantee, namely, their appeal to the reason and conscience of the individual citizen.

Our traditional ultra-individualist legal and political philosophy was confirmed by the experience of the last century, when there was a great public domain open to settlement, great natural resources were at hand open to easy individual exploitation with no need of capital, and ample opportunities for adventure were at every one's back door, involving no anti-social possibilities. The points of conflict and areas of overlapping of interests were relatively few and solution of the conflicts and adjustment of the over-lappings were usually possible with no great or detailed curtailment of individual freedom. Today, in a time when these conflicts and overlappings have increased enormously, the claim to free self-assertion is stronger and the conditions of exercising that claim are more difficult. Traditional precepts of morals and ethical custom have been undermined by the expansion of scientific knowledge. Yet while men have been emancipating themselves from these precepts, new orderings have been growing up, such as the in-

fluence of newspapers and magazines, not merely
through deliberate propaganda, but in inducing common habits of thought, common attitudes, and common understanding of things to a standard pattern,
set by their daily reading and the tendency of news
writers to standard methods. Education, too, has
tended in this direction as the enormous numbers to
be taught and the rise of standard ideas and methods
of teaching has been making for standard general
knowledge and standardized thinking.

Obviously there is a conflict here which cannot but
confuse individual conceptions of conduct. Moreover, reaction from the conditions imposed by the
standardized life demanded in our economic order,
perhaps a certain inferiority complex growing out
of it, as men compare their routine of existence with
the ideal of free self-assertion, has led to insistence
on self-assertion in the form of exceptional conduct,
of being different, of flying in the face of conven-
tions, of doing shocking things, so much in evidence
in the present century. It is worth while to compare eighteenth- with twentieth-century thinking in
this respect. The eighteenth century insisted on a
rational order of human relations. It insisted on referring all things to the measure of man in a state
of nature, of an abstract perfect man, and argued
from the universal abstract qualities of this abstract
man, not from the unique concrete demands of concrete men. It thought of conduct in terms of a universal rational order. It was exceptionally an age of
formal, artificial over-refinement of manners. Thus,

when it was possible in large measure to be individually self-sufficient, men were eager to be standard; they wished to be judged by the criterion of a standard man. Now, when an economic order based on minute division of labor and the extreme of specialization is driving them to be standard, they insist that no two are alike, they insist on the nonrational elements in conduct and that it is a series of unrelated acts or habits, they insist on individualized treatment, they claim to be judged by the measure of themselves. Law, as an avowed régime of ordering, is as irksome in the latter environment as it was theoretically acceptable in the former. It is significant that openly expressed contempt for prohibitory laws is most acute among educated, intelligent persons at the top of the social scale, among whom the conditions which make for conscious show of self-assertion are most pressing.

Not the least significant feature in the background of the legal order is the working of the more important non-legal agencies of social control. Hence, loss of efficiency in our older non-legal institutions and rise of new ones are phenomena to be brought into relation with those of the legal administration of justice. One effect of the new economic order upon our political institutions has been spoken of in another connection. But a more specific effect must be noted also. The whole direction of our urban industrial development is away from the provincialism or particularism characteristic of our inherited institutions, and even more of those we devised or reshaped for pioneer America. Those institutions, however, became fixed in response to the needs or ideals of a rural, agricultural society and so in a local, particularist mold. Indeed, the other main agency of social control in the last century, the church, became a quasi-authoritative exponent of the social norms of a pioneer, rural society, and has been showing little capacity of adaptation to the tasks of social control in the society of today. It is not easy for any institution, whose ends and tenets have been formulated to the needs of one time, in propositions taken to be of universal validity, to maintain itself when those ends cease to govern men's action.

With political, legal, and religious institutions thus largely out of tune with the times, new types of organized agencies of social control have been growing up—class, trade, business, and professional organizations of many kinds—which are playing an important part in the ordering of conduct, and yet often tend further to confuse rather than to guide intelligently, and too often have had anti-social incidental effects. For one thing, these organizations are often over class-conscious. Not infrequently, too, they fall into the hands of persons eager to make themselves permanent places by activity in the organization, who foment action simply to give it an appearance of a useful task. Most of these organizations, for either reason, are prone to bring pressure upon lawmakers and administrative officers for class and group purposes, to seek to use legislation and administration for private ends, to promote lawless laws or lawless enforcement of laws, taking their class or group ideals to be paramount to the received ideals of the legal order.   This condition of institutional inadequacy is characteristic of eras of transition.   It was felt strongly at the Reformation, in seventeenth-century England, and in the United States just after the Revolution.   Inadequate institutions function badly or indifferently, and the distrust of them, resulting from their inefficient functioning, further enfeebles them and gives rise to a vicious circle.   All social institutions are likely to be distrusted for a time and the distrust makes them less worthy of trust as judged by their workings.   Thus, in the sixteenth century we get the idea of private interpretation, in the seventeenth century we get the dogma of a "right of revolution."   In the beginning of the American polity we get the exaltation of individual liberty.   In the present we get insistence upon private judgment as to obeying laws.   The ferment of recourse to free individual self-assertion in such an era, judged by standards of the past, is likely to be held lawlessness.   Yet our fathers would have called it "liberty."   Our criminal justice should be judged in relation to the other agencies of social control in this respect, if we are to have a fair picture.

The Machinery of Criminal Justice in the Modern City

As one studies criminal justice in action in America today, he must be struck with the way in which the different agencies of justice, acting quite independently, continually hinder or thwart each other, or, if fortunately there is no interference, at best lend each other little or no aid. Each state, each county, each municipality, each court, each prosecutor, each police organization—and often more than one is operating in the same territory—is likely to go its independent course, with little or no regard for what the other is doing. It may even happen that state and federal prosecuting agencies or judicial officers may cross each other's paths and interfere with each other's operations. The well known case of Dodge, wanted in New York for perjury and fled to Texas, is an extreme but characteristic example. Before he could be taken back to New York, there were four writs of habeas corpus, there was a conflict of jurisdiction between state and federal officials, there were four extradition warrants, one injunction, one appeal, and one contempt proceeding. Even then it was necessary for a masterful detective to take the bull by the horns and put the fugitive into the hands of justice by an extra-legal coup. Nothing could illustrate better the extreme decentralization, the want of organization or coöperation, the overgrowth of checks and hindrances, and the hypertrophy of procedure which embarrass the administration of criminal justice in the economically unified land of today.

In more than one locality, local and state police may act together or may act independently, or may act at cross purposes. Federal enforcement officers acting under different bureaus have been known to

ignore or even thwart each other. State and federal
enforcement agencies frequently clash, and when
municipal, state, and federal agencies have concurrent powers, they seldom concur in any effective co-
operation. Where there is but one jurisdiction involved, police, public prosecutor and coroner may
proceed with parallel investigations, or with investigations that cross each other, or may even hamper
each other, as the exigencies of politics, quest for
publicity, or zeal for the public service may dictate.
Indeed, such things used to happen in England. In
the Baranelli case, the police and the coroner en-
gaged in an unseemly squabble for jurisdiction, such
as might happen in almost any American community
today. "The coroner," who, as we are told, "was
sensible of his privileges and duties, made out a warrant committing Baranelli to Newgate. But the
head of Scotland Yard would have none of this,
maintaining that the murderer was his property, and
not subject at all to the municipal officer. The
wretched prisoner was bundled into a cab by the coroner's two underlings, and they were about to mount
the box and drive off with their prize, when an in-
spector of police came on the scene, took command
of the box, and, seizing the reins, galloped away in
triumph." Such eminently Anglo-Saxon proceedings could not happen in England today. The same
causes, principally economic, which have led to a
better organization of the means of dealing with
crime in England, must lead us to eliminate administrative conflicts and clashes from our polity.

But the administrative anarchy of criminal justice does not stop here. I have spoken of the possibilities of a contested interstate rendition. In the case put, the Governor was willing to surrender the fugitive. Not infrequently, however, a Governor, for reasons personal to himself, will refuse to honor a requisition from the Governor of another state. Thus lack of coöperation between states may be added to lack of coöperation between the agencies of criminal investigation. Nor is there any more coöperation between the prosecuting officials within the state. In one large city recently there were repeated and long-continued controversies between the administrative officer entrusted with the enforcement of the law as to motor vehicles, the public prosecutors, and the courts, and one could not but suspect that the parties to this unhappy controversy were at least as eager to score at the other's expense as they were zealous to maintain the general security.

Things are little better in our judicial organization. The spectacle of proceedings in one court hampering or thwarting the work of justice in another court is but too common. In the Dodge case, already cited, it was carried to absurd lengths. Indeed, in any murder case of note, after conviction and affirmance upon appeal, counsel for the condemned accused make the rounds of the courts, seeking to find some judge, state or federal, willing to tie up the proceedings by some sort of judicial process. Even within the court in too many states, the judge is made quite powerless to control the trial, and the jury becomes an independent tribunal with large scope for disregarding or nullifying the law. At common law there was at least provision for coöperation between judge and jury.

At length, it may be, a criminal prosecution comes to the stage of sentence. In pioneer America, the accused was a neighbor. The judge knew him or could easily learn what was to be known, and needed no assistance. Today, on the other hand, there is peculiar need of coöperation, and yet the course of judicial action is as much at large as in pioneer times. He may utilize the information and experience of police, administrative officers, and social agencies or not, as he sees fit. Moreover, if he would use these things they are not always available nor can he always compel them to be made available. It frequently happens that while administrative officials complain of the courts for ignorant action in imposing or suspending sentence, the judges are complaining of those same officials for keeping them in ignorance. In truth, when it is no one's business to make these independent agencies work together, nothing else may be expected.

Maintenance of the general security in the close-knit economic order of today, with the new conditions of rapid transportation and easy movement across political lines, demands organization of administrative agencies, coördination of responsibility with power, and reliance upon personality rather than upon a system of checks and balances. Such things are called for in the twentieth century as emphatically as the conditions of a pioneer, rural community demanded decentralization, division of power, independent magistracies, and elaborate checks upon administration. We have become unified economically, and there must be a corresponding development in our legal institutions. If we fear centralization, we must learn to bring about coöperation.

Here is an item of the first importance in any program of improvement. Within each state we must organize the administrative agencies of criminal justice. All these agencies, including the work now done in enforcement of criminal law by sheriffs, coroners, clerks, bailiffs, and probation officers, ought to be unified under a responsible head and put in proper relation to the head of an organized judicial system, so as to eliminate friction and insure uniform policies in judicial and administrative action. But this administrative unification is not desirable beyond state lines. There we must turn to coöperation. The states have already learned in some measure to coöperate in legislation. Also the council of Governors and national associations of prosecutors, of police officials, and of those interested in penal treatment are making straight the paths. First, however, there must be unification, organization, and system within the states. When that step has been taken, coöperation between the state administrative systems will come naturally. Thus we may attain a coöperation of the preventive, administrative, prosecuting, judicial, and penal systems throughout the country, to the end that the general security be maintained through intelligent working of the machinery of criminal justice as a whole and in all its parts. The alternative is the centralization we have been taught to dread, to which a continuance of administrative anarchy may yet drive us.

Turning to the details of the machinery of criminal justice, as we took them from the last century and must use them in the modern city, and beginning at the beginning, namely, the apparatus of criminal investigation, one of the gravest difficulties is rigidity of organization, often prescribed by legislation for all municipalities. Minute legislative prescribing of detail hinders needed adjustments. In a large city it sometimes makes such elaborate provision for a "fair trial" of an accused officer as to impair or preclude discipline. Hardly less serious is lack of continuity in administration. Indeed, every part of criminal justice suffers from what Mr. Fosdick aptly calls "transient administration." This is one of the legacies of our pioneer polity. Under that polity, successive incumbents in the directing offices, need not and often do not have the same policy—or indeed formulate any policy. Each incumbent must learn anew what ought to be a known body of experience handed down from official to official and continuously adapted to new situations as they arise. But no such continuity of policy is possible, no such enlightened use of experience is possible, where the persons in charge of criminal investigation do not have assured permanence of tenure. Continuity of policy and organization of experience are precluded where there is short or precarious tenure, where choice of personnel is governed by politics, or where such choice is limited to a politico-geographical area.

Survival of pioneer ideas of versatility does much mischief here. Officials and subordinates are expected to do highly specialized tasks offhand, in a rotation of work with little adequate provision for the specialization involved in enforcement of the criminal law in a modern city. Hence there is often great lack of scientific training and consequent reliance upon quacks and charlatans, lack of knowledge of available scientific means of investigation, and, what is less excusable, lack of knowledge of the legal limitations upon prosecutions, and legal requirements as to evidence, frequently rendering futile much expenditure of effort. Nor is there any provision for intelligent study of the functioning of the apparatus of investigation either by those who operate it or by others.

In its operation, apart from the heavy burden of politics, which not infrequently impedes its workings when persons of political consequence are concerned, the machinery of criminal investigation, as we inherited it from the last century and are using it today, is marked by want of coöperation, by diffusion of responsibility, making it difficult or impossible to hold any one for unsatisfactory results, and by a tendency to develop a perfunctory routine, due to inadequate systems of supervision and to want of definitely located responsibility. When we add to these the burden of discretion as to an infinitude of minor infractions, which an individual police officer must bear under the conditions of the time, and the burdens growing from our treatment of all breaches of administrative regulations as crimes, it is indeed worthy of wonder that our system is still on the whole so adequate in its workings as to maintain an average security of life and limb and property.

Nowhere do pioneer ideas of decentralization, diffusion of responsibility, and versatility do so much mischief as in our prosecuting system. The district attorney (or state's attorney or prosecuting attorney—he bears these and other names in different jurisdictions) combines the functions of criminal investigator (more or less concurrent with coroner and sheriff or police), of the common-law attorney general exercising discretion as to whether a private prosecution shall go on, of a solicitor preparing the case for trial, and of an advocate trying the case in court. In a modern city such a diversity of functions requires a highly organized office, with permanent personnel, intelligent division of labor, definite allocation of responsibility, and an efficient system of records. One need only compare the organization or want of organization of the average office of a prosecutor in one of our large cities with that of the average legal department of a public service company having no more and no more important litigation, to understand a large factor in the ineffectiveness of American criminal justice of today. In many great urban centers, the district attorney's office still goes on after the manner of the old-time country law

office, where relatively few causes were to be tried at
periodical terms with intervals between them, although the most ordinary office doing a civil business
is organized on modern lines for communities in
which courts have enormous calendars and are continuously in session. The usual way of meeting the
increased volume of business is to add more assistants. But to conduct such an office efficiently there
must be system and organization. The office must be
put in relation to a responsible central agency; it
must have a permanent, even if flexible, organization
and to some extent, at least, a permanent personnel
removed from politics. There must be intelligent
segregation of cases as well as numerous assistants.

Undoubtedly the bane of prosecution in the United
States of today is the intimate connection of the
prosecutor's office with politics. The sinews of war
for local political rings in our cities are derived
chiefly from organized or exploited vice, and organized or exploited law breaking. The position of
public prosecutor is politically strategic in the highest degree. It plays directly into the hands of these
rings when the prosecutor is elected for a relatively
short term and his assistants are political appointees
likewise with short tenure of their positions. If the
prosecutor is ambitious, he looks upon his office as a
stepping stone to Congress or to the Governorship.
This does not mean that he must strive to carry out
his tasks efficiently, but that he must carry them out
conspicuously. "Making a record" for political
purposes bears no necessary relation to effective

prosecution of the everyday work of his office. For example, prosecutors publish statements showing "convictions" running to thousands each year. But more than ninety per cent. of these "convictions" are upon pleas of guilty, made on "bargain days," in the assured expectation of nominal punishment, as the cheapest way out, and amounting in effect to license to violate the law. The political value of sensation and the danger of offending those on whose political favor he must depend for political advancement, are not unlikely to drive him to a perfunctory routine for his ordinary work and spectacular handling of a few sensational cases.

This subjection of prosecution to politics is made the worse by the want of organization and system in prosecution, by the want of continuity in office, by the want of adequate checks upon what is done and what not and why, and by the lack hitherto of any adequate and continuous study of how far the régime of prosecution actually achieves its ends and where and how and why it falls short. Want of any effective central head to the prosecuting system as a whole, either state or local, diffused responsibility, and ill defined responsibility, play into the hands of the professional defenders, who are mostly deep in politics. Want of continuity of personnel, want of any continuous experience, at all comparable to that of the professional defenders, and the rapid turnover among assistants as well as at the head, are also all to the advantage of the professional defenders. If, upon other grounds, our polity requires the periodical election of state prosecutors—which is at least debatable—a high degree of permanent organization in the office and a minimum permanent personnel under the civil service are clearly indicated as correctives. One needs only note the work of the small staff of veteran prosecutors in the United States Department of Justice to see the possibilities of a properly selected permanent personnel.

Political responsibility was a check on the prosecutor in a proper sense in pioneer America, where dockets were small, where the citizens in large and representative numbers attended all trials, where every one knew what the prosecutor did and how and why. Political responsibility kept him from doing what he should not. Nowadays politics are a check in an improper sense, hindering him from doing what he should. Today, political pressure upon prosecutions, except in rare intervals of political upheaval, is a weapon against society, not a shield of the innocent individual citizen.

Taking up the course of a prosecution in detail, the prosecutor may or may not take a hand in criminal investigation, either generally or in particular cases. His duties in this respect are not clearly defined and responsibility as between sheriff or police and prosecutor is, as usual, divided or diffused. When a sensational crime has been committed, coroner, police, and district attorney may each go out for glory or publicity in their own way. Politics require taking advantage of possibilities of publicity. Thus those possibilities become a determining factor in criminal investigation. Under our legal system the way of the prosecutor is hard, and the need of "getting results" puts pressure upon prosecutors to use the "third degree," to suppress evidence, to bull-doze witnesses, and generally to indulge in that law-less enforcement of law which produces a vicious circle of disrespect for law. Yet in causes involving few possibilities of publicity they may be perfunc-tory and supine, with no check upon the resulting inefficiency.

One of the most difficult problems connected with prosecution has to do with bail, so vital to the inno-cent, so fraught with possibilities of abuse in the hands of organized malefactors backed by politics. But here, too, the pressure of politics vitiates the best of paper programs of improvement when put into action. Pressure from politicians, from surety com-panies, from professional bondsmen, which no politi-cal officer can ignore in the intervals of public wrath, make for a lax administration of any system, with intervals of drastic severity in which the weight often falls upon the just.

Throughout the course of a prosecution the exig-encies of politics urge utilizing of the opportunities of publicity at the expense of efficiency, and the lack of organization and central responsible supervision and absence of any system of records, other than the formal record of the court, afford temptation to use the mitigating agencies, in which criminal procedure abounds, as means of covering up or of "passing the buck." The grand jury has long outlived its use-

fulness. But the way in which causes are presented
to that body may make its power of ignoring indict-
ments useful under the pressure of politics. Where
the number of prosecutions each year has become
enormous—far beyond possibilities of trial—the
common-law unlimited power of *nol. pros.* becomes a
means of selection of those to be prosecuted, of which
politicians have not been slow to take advantage.
Originally this was a public check upon private
prosecutions. Now, it is not a check upon a power,
but a power needing check, and thus far the statutory
checks provided in some of our states have operated
perfunctorily and achieved little.

Again, in the trial of causes the desire to make a
"record" too often controls at the expense of efficiency and to the neglect of legitimate interests secured by law. The prosecutor will be seen leading in
man hunts, requiring new trials, the odium of which
falls on the higher courts instead of on the prosecutor who knew better. The number of new trials
for grave misconduct of the public prosecutor which
may be found in the reports throughout the land
in the past two decades is significant. We must go
back to the seventeenth century—to the trial of
Raleigh or to the prosecutions under Jeffreys—to
find parallels for the abuse and disregard of forensic
propriety which threatens to become staple in American prosecutions. No fifth wheel of a public de-
fender will avail so long as the public prosecutor is
under such strong temptation to be spectacular. One
has only to compare the excess of zeal at the trial

with the perfunctory way in which the same public prosecutor will present his case before the appellate tribunal, where no reporters are at hand, to see what is really meant by responsibility of the prosecutor to "the people." There are prosecutors everywhere who are honorable exceptions. But even the best, with their paths made hard by our inherited criminal law and procedure, are likely to be caught in the cogs of a bad system.

Any program for bettering our administration of criminal justice must seek to take prosecutions out of politics, to centralize control of them in each state under some sort of director of public prosecutions with secure tenure and concentrated and defined responsibility, and to provide some sort of ministry of justice in each state, to study the workings of the system, find out what it does and wherein it fails and how and why, and study how to make it more effective.

Nothing could be more foreign to the conditions in which courts sit today than those for which our judicial organization was laid out in the eighteenth and fore part of the nineteenth century. Then decentralization was called for, as organization and unification are called for today. In England, in 1873, there was a complete reorganization which went far in the direction of unification. In the federal judicial system much has been done in that direction. Some few states have moved cautiously toward unification and some few had from the beginning a certain unification, potential at least, of their courts of first instance. But the standard American judicial organization is a hierarchy of distinct courts, involving waste of judicial power, waste of time and money in elaborate proceedings to get from one tribunal to another, and elaborate appellate procedure. What we must chiefly consider in connection with criminal justice is the courts of first instance. Here we find usually the overlappings of jurisdiction, the ill defined powers, the diffusion of responsibility characteristic of our pioneer institutions. Multiplication of judges and patchwork adaptation have been the chief means by which to meet a situation which calls for thorough reorganization. Multiplication of judges, without unification of the judicial system, makes of each court of general jurisdiction not an organized entity with systematized business methods, controlled by a responsible head on an intelligently determined policy, but a congeries of coordinate tribunals, each proceeding as if it had before it its own small volume of business, as in pioneer days; as if it had the intimate personal knowledge of the men and things before it, and was subject to the check of general knowledge of those men and things by the whole community, which obtained even in the large town or small city of the middle of the last century.

Next to unification of the judicial system as a whole, there is call for adequate provision for petty prosecutions. It is here that the administration of criminal justice touches immediately the greatest number of people. It is here that the great mass of

an urban population, whose experience of law is too
likely to have been only an experience of arbitrary
discretion of police officers and offhand action of
magistrates, tempered by political influence, might
be taught the spirit of our institutions and made to
feel that the law was a living force for securing their
interests. Such things as the mass disposition of
liquor prosecutions in the federal courts in our large
cities do much harm to the legal order, yet are inevitable as those courts and their business are organized. Even in the modern municipal courts in
some of our large cities, the physical conditions and
decorum are often those of the old-time police court
of a small town, when the police magistrate knew the
town drunkard, as did all his neighbors, and could
dispose of the case of Huck Finn's father offhand,
with the assurance of one who knew. The methods of
the rural magistrate are out of place without the
personal knowledge on the part of the court and the
community which they presuppose. Without this
check, there are opportunities for questionable influences in the case of real offenders and in danger of
irreparable injury to the occasional offender who is
not able to command such influences. The bad physical surroundings, the confusion, the want of decorum,
the undignified offhand disposition of cases at high
speed, the frequent suggestion of something working behind the scenes, which characterize the petty
criminal court in almost all of our cities, create in
the minds of observers a general suspicion of the

whole process of law enforcement which, no matter how unfounded, gravely prejudices the law.

There is no less need of reconsidering our established polity with respect to the personnel, tenure, and mode of choice of judges. Where judges are chosen by direct primary followed by popular election, the need of keeping in the public eye, in order to insure re-election, has made the judicial Barnum a characteristic feature of the American bench. When judges were made elective, in the middle of the last century, every one could and probably did know the character and qualifications of the few conspicuous lawyers who were candidates for judicial office in the judicial district, or of the rising young lawyers who sought election as police magistrates in the town. The more citizens that voted, the more intelligent the choice. But today the average city dweller can know the judges and lawyers only from the newspapers. Those whose names are most frequently in the papers are by no means the best qualified, and it is not unlikely that the greater the number of citizens who vote, the more unintelligent the choice. Those best qualified are likely to shrink from candidacy for judicial office in view of what it involves in the city of today.

It cannot be said too often or too emphatically that the judiciary has, on the whole, the best record of any of our institutions. This, however, is due largely to a tradition which has shown signs of disappearing under the untoward conditions of our urban centers.

The high-water mark of corruption under the Tweed
régime in the last century is rightly regarded as exceptional. But something very like it is appearing
in petty courts, and even in criminal courts of first
instance, in more than one large city of the present.
What is worse, mediocrity, timidity, susceptibility to
political pressure and influence, the usual concomi-
tants of an elective bench in metropolitan cities,
create suspicion of corruption where it does not exist.
The advertising judge, the spectacular judge, the
judicial "good fellow," the judge who caters to
groups and societies and identifies himself with racial
and religious and trade organizations, has much to
do with the ineffectiveness of the machinery of justice. Such judges are all but unknown to the federal
bench, although there have been federal judicial ap-
pointments on the basis of politics and the Senate
has pushed hard to make federal judicial appoint-
ments a matter of patronage. They are all but unknown, despite the contagion of the bad example of
the country at large, in a few jurisdictions where the
common-law tradition of an independent bench still
obtains. Nowhere is a wholly independent bench so
needed as in the large city of today. If it is imperative to divorce prosecution from politics, it is no less
imperative to divorce the bench from politics. If the
régime of judges appointed for life, which gave us
the great judges who made our law, cannot be re-
stored, we must learn to use our nominating and
electing machinery to ratify a choice made on non-
political lines by those who are competent to select,

and must make tenure secure.   Indeed, there are signs
that pressure of the economic order has begun to lead
toward something of this sort in more than one state.

In the last quarter of the nineteenth century, except for typically rural jurisdictions, the organization of the profession which had grown up for pioneer America was manifestly becoming inadequate.
In the present, predominantly urban, century, it is
responsible for much of the shortcomings of our
criminal justice. The criminal courts in large cities
are frequently without proper assistance from competent prosecutors and defenders. The standards of
forensic conduct and of preparation of prosecution
and defense are often lax and even bad. The public
gets a wrong idea of law and of law enforcement
from what seems to be tolerated, if not matter-of-
course conduct on the part of the practitioners with
whom they come in contact in the courts.

Even when professional conduct was at a relatively
low level in England, the upper branch of the profession was held to standards of character and conduct through the Inns of Court. The lower branch
could in the last century show such persons as Samp-
son Brass and Caleb Quirk of Alibi House—well
known types in the American city of today. But the
solicitors also were organized in the nineteenth century, and the lower branch of the profession has been
put on a high plane through the Incorporated Law
Society and like organizations. With us, bar associations grew up in the last quarter of the nineteenth
century and have been having a notable development

in the present century. Yet, except for a few states, which have incorporated the profession, membership in such associations is voluntary, and those most in need of the restraint which membership therein would afford are not eligible. A movement for organization of the profession as a whole has just begun. Out of these experiments should come presently a real profession, adapted to the conditions of the time, where now we have no more than so many thousand or so many hundred lawyers, pursuing a money-making calling, each as he pleases, and answerable only to their own consciences. Centralized admission under the auspices of the highest court of the state, is a step in the right direction, taken in most jurisdictions during the present century. This, however, is only a small beginning.

There never was a check in the organization of the profession in this country. A great change has taken place with respect to the check involved in preliminary and professional training. In pioneer America the lawyer served an apprenticeship in an office and by the time he was ready to come to the bar was well known to those who vouched for him to their fellow practitioners. But any real apprentice training long ago became impossible except here and there where old-time rural law offices still obtain. Today the great bulk of the profession is school trained. This change is inevitable in the economic order of the time and has great possibilities. Unhappily, there are all varieties of law schools, from the university law school, well endowed, well equipped, with high stan-

dards of admission and severe standards of gradua-
tion, to money-making schools, conducted as private
enterprises, with few facilities and merely nominal
standards, seeking no more than to train for the local
bar examinations.   The upper stratum of the legal
profession in the United States is at least as well
trained as the profession in any part of the world.
But in our cities there is a numerous and increasing
lower stratum, little educated or uneducated, often
with little or no grasp of the language, with no grasp
of the historical background of our institutions,
trained superficially in night schools in rule-of-thumb
procedure.   What this means for criminal justice was
brought out in the Cleveland Survey.   The students
from the night schools, who went out to practise in
the criminal courts, had given one third as much time
to criminal law as was required in the three university
law schools in the state from those who were to practise chiefly on the civil side.   Except for cases of
great magnitude, practice in the criminal courts has
mostly fallen into the hands of this lower stratum,
with the result, among others, that the common-law
mitigating agencies, meant to be checks, have come to
require checks and are in effect without any.

Judicial discipline of lawyers is not self-operating.
It must be invoked.   With a small local bar, in which
every one knew every one else and what he was doing,
it sufficed for the rare cases in which formal discipline
was needed.   With an enormous roll of practitioners
in every city, it is impossible for the leaders to know
more than a small fraction of their fellow lawyers,

much less to have any adequate information as to
what they are doing. The grievance committees of
bar associations, as a matter of public spirit, have
been doing good work in many places in setting the
disciplinary machinery in motion. The work is, however, invidious and time-consuming, and no one is
responsible for keeping it up at a high level of efficiency. What is everybody's business tends to be
nobody's business. The check of judicial discipline
has been weakened to the point of ineffectiveness.

Even more is this true of the check of daily association at circuit and daily appearance in court.
The circuit bar has disappeared with modern conditions of travel. Many of the best lawyers never
appear in court. Many more appear but rarely.
The habitual practitioners in criminal cases do not
operate as a check; they need a check. Conditions
of practice today have made the check involved in the
old-time association of lawyers in and out of court,
and of relations between judges and lawyers in and
out of court, substantially obsolete. At common law
the bar was a check on the courts and the courts were
a check on the bar. Unhappily, in large cities
neither of these reciprocal checks is longer of much
avail. We must develop new ones, apparently
through some organization of the profession in each
state, with a higher level of education, both general
and professional, and definite centralized responsibility for the conduct of each practitioner.

Nineteenth-century America took the lead in the
development of penal treatment. Unhappily just at

the time when some of the best products of American
inventive genius in this connection were coming into
use, the transition to an urban industrial order began
to throw a heavy strain upon the administration of
criminal justice. Before these new institutions could
be well worked out, before they could be fitted into
our old machinery, before judges everywhere appre-
ciated them, and before a body of experts had been
trained to work them, the public, dissatisfied with the
palpable inefficiency of our criminal justice in urban
centers, began to charge the ill-workings of the whole
system upon these innovations. Undoubtedly there
were abuses and the provisions for administration
were frequently inadequate. But despite insufficient
personnel and facilities, despite the infection of politics in many jurisdictions, despite routine methods in
a connection where routine is out of order, and in
spite of the suspicion which has been cast upon it and
so has impeded its operations, our system of probation and its analogues is one of the outstanding good
features of our criminal justice.

Penal treatment in America today raises specially
difficult questions because the time calls for individualization and the traditional spirit of our law
calls for generalized penalties; because our ideas,
inherited from the last century, are characteristically
humane and stress the individual life, while the times
demand greater regard for the general security; because at a time when we need to experiment and try
out new devices the public fears a relaxation of punitive measures; because conditions of urban life and a

multitude of new offenses have filled our penal institutions with types for which our traditional methods are ill-adapted, and yet new methods are scouted as depriving penal treatment of its deterrent effect. Adequately treated, the subject would call for a lecture of itself. It is enough to say that the prospect here is much more immediately hopeful than at any other point in American criminal justice. We are less in a rut here. A body of trained workers has been growing up which thoroughly understands the problem, its history, and its present status. We are less hampered here than elsewhere by the pioneer tradition and by pioneer institutions. Penal treatment is not unlikely to continue to be characteristically the American field of progress in criminal law and administration.

The Obstacles to Improvement

As one reads the discussions in the reports of bar associations he can but feel that a chief obstacle to improvement is in the democratic tradition; in what we must pronounce false ideas of democracy. Throwing of even the least details of all things into politics and subjection of every one and everything to political pressure are traditional American ideals. But are they not pioneer ideals rather than necessarily democratic ideals? Is it inevitably required that an urban industrial democracy have the same polity in all respects as a rural, agricultural democracy? No doubt the "cult of incompetency" has been everywhere an unhappy by-product of democracy. But the pressure of the economic order is forcing Demos to choose better counselors and better servants. Distrust of judges, lay magistrates, free rein to counsel in the forum, extravagant powers of juries, an uneducated, unorganized, deprofessionalized bar are urged as democratic, and their supposed democratic character is expected to make up for their manifest inadaptation to the demands of justice today. Every proposal to make our administration of justice more effective is resisted eloquently in the name of the common people, or of justice to the poor and oppressed. But these are pioneer institutions, not necessarily democratic institutions. There is no intrinsic reason why democratic institutions should be inefficient. In eras of transition, aristocratic or autocratic institutions have also been known to be inefficient. Pioneer institutions were democratic. It does not follow that democratic institutions must be those of the pioneer. Moreover, the people at large suffer most from a condition of ineffective justice. Great enterprises, with highly organized legal staff, are much better able to secure their interests under such a system than is the average man. The poor and oppressed are not better off by being left to the risk of ignorant or unscrupulous practitioners. The legal aid societies in our cities tell a significant story. If democracy involves regard for the interests of the mass of humanity, petty justice in our cities falls far short of its demands. Demos must learn to govern urban America by means adapted to its problems.

He cannot expect to go on governing by means suited only to the pioneer America which has disappeared.

Another obstacle, it may as well be said frankly, will be found in the attitude of the press in the United States toward criminal investigation, prosecution, and trial. No doubt desire of those charged with investigation and prosecution, and even sometimes of judges, to obtain a maximum of continuous publicity, may not be overlooked. But the commercial value of dramatic news items has pushed public considerations into the background. It has made us callous to infringements of private rights, as one may see by comparing the consequences of libel in England with those in the United States. Even more it has made us forgetful of the public interests involved in newspaper discussion of pending cases. In the United States the press insists on trying cases in its columns. In England, as one may see from the Tibbets case, punishment would follow at once for what American newspapers do every day in case of crimes attracting general notice. The practice of the American press adds greatly to the difficulty of getting a fair trial, and explains much of the delay in obtaining juries, which is so often reprehended. We must remember this in any comparison of English with American criminal trials.

Also we must bear in mind the great difference between the accurate, often expert accounts of the facts of trials, which appear in the English press, and the flippant, typically sensational, and often legally ignorant accounts in the American press.

With us the newspapers stress the incidents at the expense of the proceeding as a whole. They recount clashes between counsel, bits of testimony which may be made amusing, tilts between counsel and witnesses, and the like, giving a sketch, which is often a caricature, rather than a true picture, featuring it as a spectacle instead of as what it is. It is not merely that this makes for pressure upon judges and prosecutors who are elective officers to neglect efficiency and furnish material for headlines. Effective justice requires public understanding and approval of what goes on in the courts. In fact, our criminal trials are much better than the average press account makes them appear. A radical change in newspaper methods is needed if our criminal justice is to be more effective.

A third obstacle which will long stand in the way of improvement is to be found in the organization of the legislature in most states, dating from a rural, agricultural era and giving a decided preponderance to localities in which older and now obsolescent conditions obtain. The chief difficulties in criminal justice are in the cities or about the metropolitan areas. But for the greater part of what a great city needs in order to cope with crime, it must depend on action by the state legislature or even on amendments to the state constitution. In the end, the state may do anything not forbidden it by the federal constitution. The state legislature may do anything not prohibited to it by the federal and state constitutions. The city, on the other hand, may do only what the state empowers it to do. Although it is typical and normal in the social and economic life of today, legally it is treated as something exceptional, as it was in the pioneer polity. In order to adapt the institutions devised for the conditions of the past to the rapidly changing urban conditions of the time, the city must induce action by those who live substantially under the older conditions, to whom the methods and agencies developed for rural communities of the last century seem to be working well enough. Much which is laid to innate conservatism of lawyers, is really attributable to inability or disinclination of the best country lawyers to appreciate the legal and administrative problems of the large cities, re-inforced by the mass of ill-trained lawyers in those cities, who conceive of law in terms of procedural rules. The leaders of the bar in our cities have long been going forward in the movement for better things. It is not so much conservatism of lawyers which stands in the way of improvement as the conditions under which the lawyers who make up the strength of the legislatures live and practise.

Where there are a number of large cities in a state, each with its own problems, and a large agricultural population with preponderant political power, proper provision for the needs of criminal justice in the cities becomes a matter of much difficulty. Probably the solution lies in a unified judicial organization for the whole state, a state ministry of justice, and an organization of the administrative agencies of justice for the whole state. Such an organization of justice, under a head responsible for insuring an adequate functioning of the legal system in each locality, and clothed with power to make the proper adjustments to that end, might from time to time, as occasion required, bring about the right compromises between urban and rural needs. It could preserve the balance between city and country, as changes take place, without disturbing the fundamental organization. As things are, the perennial suspicion and even hostility between the two elements in the economic life of the state constantly obstruct effective measures for a better treatment of crime.

With the passing of nineteenth-century political philosophy and the standardization involved in the minute organization of business and industry, the propensity to needless regimentation of conduct by means of the criminal law is likely to prove another serious obstacle to improvement. Organized meddling with individual conduct and even individual belief and opinion by extra-legal self-appointed groups, more hateful than any official control, and powerful to deny the legal protection which the law books purport to guarantee to the individual, has always been a characteristic feature of American life. In the present century it has increasingly affected legislation and administration. Extra-legal censorship in some parts of the country avails itself of administrative machinery and becomes at least quasi-legal. Municipal power to guard against fire, to guard against accident, and to keep the streets free and safe for traffic are used to prevent handbills, public meetings, or processions in advocacy of economic, social, or even religious views of which a mayor or a police commissioner or chief of police chances to disapprove. Courts have had to remind administrative officers, charged with the granting and revoking of permits for the conduct of manufacture, that they were not censors of the personal morals of the permittees, but only of the consonance of their conduct of their business with the rules applicable thereto. The power to legislate for the public health, safety, and morals is stretching to cover a multitude of interferences with the individual life which go beyond any reasoned adjustment of the individual life and the general security. Such, to take an example which can hardly be controversial, were the anti-cigarette laws of two decades ago. So long as the criminal law has to carry the burden of enforcing such regulations, which do not appeal strongly to any beyond the insistent group which secures their enactment, it is sure to be strained in its administration, and the strain at this point will affect the whole system.

The Agencies of Improvement

It will have been seen that many of our difficulties are quite beyond the reach of formal lawmaking. They lie in our social, political, and legal history and have to do with settled frames of mind and received attitudes toward the legal order. They must be overcome by a slow process of disappearance of pioneer modes of thought, of developing ideas of

social life and establishing ideals of conduct and of
the relation of each to his fellows appropriate to an
urban, industrial society. There must be a strength-
ening of the old restraining agencies, which formerly
shared with law the burden of social control, but are
now weakened under the social and economic conditions of the time, or else the setting up of new ones.
There must be a stabilizing of the economic order,
which for a time has been going forward too rapidly
for the law to keep pace with it. Only then can there
be a stabilizing of ethical custom, and thus a firm
background for criminal justice. There must be a
readjustment of political institutions to conform to
economic realities. There must be a social psychological adjustment, an adjustment of social life to
the new inventions, a stabilizing of wants, an individual adjustment to propaganda, advertising, and
salesmanship as promotives of unrest, an adjustment
of beliefs and opinions to the unsettling conceptions
of modern science, just as it was needful to adjust
when Galileo displaced the earth as the center of the
universe, or when Darwin upset fixed views as to
man's place in nature. Very likely there must be further development of voluntary associations—business, trade, professional, and fraternal—so as to fit
better into the scheme of modern life.

Such developments are going on. The forces
which make for a better understanding of each part
of the land by every other, and of each man, each
group, each class, by every other, are acting upon
the old formulas and giving them new content; are

acting rapidly and effectively upon the old prejudices and old attitudes. Cheap and quick transportation, general going about in automobiles, the radio,
the general diffusion of news, enabling comparison of
locality with locality and bringing out some picture
of a whole, are dissipating pioneer provincialism and
relaxing pioneer modes of thought, and thus are making for unification and coöperation. Along with
these, education and the pressure of the exigencies of
the economic order must go before the formal agencies of improvement and give them direction and
guidance.

What formal agencies are at hand to remake our
substantive criminal law, reshape our criminal procedure, reorganize our prosecuting machinery, and
make our courts and our penal treatment more effective for their purposes? The staple agency has been
legislation.

It is easy to decry legislative lawmaking. It is
easy to declaim against the "rain of law." But legislative lawmaking is obviously the type of lawmaking
of the maturity of law. If we are inclined to scoff
at it, we should remember that legislation solved the
problem of workmen's compensation when judicial
empiricism failed. The needs of modern business preclude waiting for a slow process of judicial inclusion
and exclusion to work out legal conceptions for many
a settled practice of manufacturing and marketing.
As the high-powered motor vehicle requires us to
mark out the middle of the road and mark zones of
safety and street crossings and turns, so the high-

pressure operations of modern business require lines to be laid out and permissible courses of conduct to be indicated in advance by legislation rather than after the event by judicial determination of controversies. We must resort to legislation. Yet admittedly legislation is most unsatisfactory in practice.

Under the circumstances of today, lawmaking calls for specialized knowledge and expert guidance. But scientific, uninterested exposition of the background of social fact and reliable uninterested guidance are seldom at hand. There is constant pressure from well organized interests with carefully prepared showings from their private standpoints. In legal matters bar associations are now doing much, sometimes very well. But all the interests to be considered are not always represented in those organizations. Formerly we relied on the lawyers in the judiciary committees of the two houses. Today those committees are not unlikely to prove obstructive only. They are frequently dominated by country lawyers, are suspicious of all unfamiliar proposals, and are content with petty changes of details of procedure at points which have come under the individual notice of their members. This tendency to mere patchwork tinkering is aggravated by the activities of organized businesses and trades. Every business, every trade, every interest has its legislative committee with a budget of approved bills to be urged upon each legislative session. These bills are drawn only with reference to what affects the particular organized interest. Thus measures enacted at the same session are not always in accord. Evils are corrected but partially, and not always consistently. Meanwhile grave defects, which do not immediately affect some such organization, remain untouched.

There has been much improvement of late. Bill drafting experts, reference bureaus, code commissions and statute commissions have done some good things. Occasionally special committees or commissions achieve something more complete and consistent for some particular field. But there is always danger that abuses will be left to themselves until a sensational event stimulates the legislative steamroller and an offhand application of lay "common sense" introduces new difficulties. This feature of legislative lawmaking, of which the classical example is the so-called reform of procedure in the middle of the last century, has given rise to much of the prejudice against legislation which prevails in the legal profession.

Two points deserve to be emphasized. It was a distinct mistake when, in the middle of the last century, legislatures, in a wave of exasperation at the disinclination of the legal profession to take up reform of procedure, began to prescribe the minute details of the conduct of proceedings in the courts. No such mistake has been made in the present generation with respect to the procedure of administrative tribunals. But the habit of legislative dictation of the minutiæ of judicial procedure dies hard. The process of legislative rule making is too dilatory, too cumbersome, too ill-informed, too subject to pressure from organizations representing but a fragment of the interests involved, to be suited to the needs of today. Judicial rule making, especially with the aid of judicial councils, is the line of advance for procedure. For the rest, a ministry of justice, charged with and responsible for study of the effects of the law in action and discovery of how far it succeeds and how far it falls short or fails of its purposes, has the greatest possibilities. Such ministries have existed for a long time in Continental Europe, and have done much to keep the administration of justice at a high level. They were advocated for the English-speaking world by Bentham and by Lord Westbury. Recently the plan was urged for England by Lord Haldane. In this country it has received the approval of a strong commission in New York and has been advocated by Judge Cardozo. We must give over the pioneer faith that the legislature is self-sufficient for things in the province of the expert. We must come to this or to some like device for securing continuous, scientific, uninterested study of the workings of the law and guidance to lawmakers in amending it.

Next to legislation, our law looks to judicial decision as a creative and amending agency. But judicial decision creates and amends here and there, incidentally and interstitially. Changes along broad lines call for legislation. Moreover, judicial decision is most effective in the field of substantive law. As things are, this agency can do little for us. The criminal law has become so thoroughly statutory as to leave little scope for judicial development. Within the narrow limits open to them, the courts labor under three serious handicaps. In the first place, the pressure of work in the appellate courts of today is enormous, both absolutely and relatively to what they were asked to do in the classical era when they made over our law. No court today can give the time to hearing exhaustive argument or take the time for elaborate consideration which was possible one hundred years ago. In those days, Story could sit in the Supreme Court of the United States at Washington, sit at circuit in Boston, and be Dane Professor of Law at Harvard. Today any one of these three tasks would exhaust his whole time and energies. The weight of judicial work hinders judicial development of the law, both on the civil and on the criminal side. But two further difficulties operate specially on the criminal side. Judicial empiricism as an agency of growth calls for the joint efforts of court and counsel. If causes are not well argued by counsel, the work of the court is likely to fall off in quality. Unhappily, in the general run of criminal cases, taking the country over, counsel fall far short of the standard which is maintained for civil cases. What is worse, when we compare the criminal with the civil side, there is the same lack of good guidance from books and juristic writing.

Something has been said about juristic science and the criminal law in another connection. Unfortunately the backwardness of juristic science with respect to criminal justice is of long standing. Criminal law was relatively neglected by the Roman jurists and in antiquity did not attain the systematic development reached by the civil side of the law. In consequence, it got a late start in the modern world, and has lagged behind conspicuously in American writing. Nowhere is the need of the highest type of juristic writing so acute as in the criminal law. Nowhere does there seem so little prospect of it. Until criminal law is studied as zealously and scientifically, and is regarded by teachers, writers, students, lawyers, and judges as being as worthy of their best and most intelligent efforts as is the civil side of the law, the administration of criminal justice is likely to continue to fall short of public expectation.

In another aspect, however, the science of law gives much promise. One of its conspicuous achievements in the present century has been a movement for unification of the social sciences, a movement to utilize the results of economics, politics, sociology, and social psychology and to develop research methods in which the other social sciences coöperate. Research of this sort is beginning to go forward in more than one place and has great possibilities. Another achievement has been the development of a functional attitude, a study of law in action as well as law in the books, an insistence upon justice through rules in contrast to abstractly just rules, an insistence upon the limitations on effective legal action, and the importance of making legal precepts effect their purposes. This sort of science of law may be made to do great things in the domain of criminal law. The two movements in recent jurisprudence should be directed to that subject energetically, as only law schools can direct them. The best minds in our law schools should be at work to discover how and how far the criminal law actually secures the social interests which we expect it to secure. They should be studying how far in practice it is possible to secure these interests by means of the criminal law. They should be studying how criminal law and judicial administration thereof may be made to do that part of the task of maintaining and furthering civilization for which they are fitted, and of which they are capable, and how they may do this in the most effective way and with the least sacrifice of the social interest in the individual life. We should not wait for ministries of justice to be set up to begin this work. The calling of the universities to this task is as clear as their calling to research in chemistry, in engineering, in medicine. The condition of our criminal law calls for continuous intelligent bringing to bear, upon the fundamental problem and its applications in detail, of all that legal and social, and psychological and medical science have worked out. Nowhere can this be done so well as in the universities and in university law schools.

The Aims of a Program of Improvement

If I am right in assuming as the crux of the situation that institutions and doctrines and precepts devised or shaped for rural or small-town conditions are failing to function efficiently under metropolitan conditions, that institutions and methods which were effective in a background of pioneer modes of thought and rural conceptions of social life in the past century are working badly in a background of modes of thought born of a developed industrial society and urban conceptions of social life in the present century, it is apparent that a great part of any program of improvement is out of the field of the lawyer and must be left to the political and social philosopher. But the lawyer's share in such a program must be large. He best knows the materials which are to be reshaped. He must find how to reshape them to the patterns drawn by philosophy and the social sciences.

No doubt a reasonable observance, a reasonable enforcement of all laws is the most to which we can attain. We may expect nothing more than a high average of observance and enforcement. Our ultimate aim must be a body of laws adequate to securing social interests and capable of that high average. But three special ends should be kept in view in the endeavor to reach this ultimate aim under the conditions of the time, namely, preventive justice, a system of individualized treatment of offenders, and a readjustment of our legally received ideals as to the balance between the general security and the individual life.

Preventive criminal justice was spoken of at length in the first lecture. It is enough to say here that at this point we need the fullest team play between legal and other social agencies, between jurisprudence and the other social sciences, between lawyers and social workers. Moreover, we need the same creative spirit and inventive activity which Americans and American lawyers displayed so abundantly in the formative period of our institutions. Indeed, the development of probation and of the juvenile court show that this inventiveness is not exhausted.

As to systematized individualization, the very conception of law, of a government of laws and not of men, calls for system, while the whole trend of psychology and penology indicates individualization, making the penal treatment fit the offender, dealing with the dangerous man rather than the dangerous act, as the line of progress. Here again is a problem in which there must be coöperation of social scientist, psychologist, physician, and lawyer. Indeed, the philosopher may well contribute, for this problem runs back to one which is fundamental in social, in legal, in penal philosophy. It comes to the problem of the division of labor and allocation of activities in a complex society, reconciled with that spontaneous initiative and free quest for individual ends which is a main source of progress.

In criminal law this problem takes the form of quest for a workable balance between the general security and the individual life. And here the lawyer is confronted with a task of reshaping the received ideals which came into the common law in the seventeenth century. We have seen that, for historical reasons, the common law emphasized the individual life at the expense of the general security, and that this overemphasis was reinforced by the social and economic and political conditions of pioneer America. Our whole apparatus of juristic thinking on this subject must be overhauled. We are not compelled to choose, as has been assumed, between a régime of atomistic individualism or one of state omnicompetence and concentration of all powers and functions in politically ordered society. Our ideas in this connection have been confused by loose use of the words "individualism" and "socialism." The juristic thinking of today must transcend both nineteenth-century individualism and nineteenth-century socialism. The orthodox natural-rights individualism is as obsolete as the orthodox Marxian socialism. Instead of valuing all things in terms of individual personality, or in terms of politically organized society, we are valuing them in terms of civilization, of raising human powers to their highest possible unfolding— toward which spontaneous free individual action and collective organized effort both contribute. As this mode of thinking becomes general, the paths of criminal justice will be made straight.

INDEX

Adams, John, 137
Administration, contrasted with
  law, 59
  function of, 29
  judicial supervision of, 98
  lack of continuity in, 180
  of justice, difficulties in, 36 ff.
  of justice, scientific standards
    in, 45
  pioneer jealousy of, 24, 87,
    150
  Puritan aversion to, 24
  unification of, 179
Administrative agencies, organ-
  ization of, 202-3
Administrative functions, dif-
  erentiation of judicial from,
  86
Administrative justice, 28-9, 39,
  132
Administrative lawlessness,
  203-4
Administrative machinery, in-
  adequacy of, 13
Administrative régime, Ameri-
  can, 149
Administrative tribunals, 49
Administrative violation of
  guaranteed rights, 53
Admiralty, 118-19
Advocates, 155-6
"Age of reason," 115
Alienists, 127-8
American administrative ré-
  gime, 149
American Bar Association, 11
American Colonies, 39
American Institute of Criminal
  Law and Criminology, 11
American judicial organization,
  99-100

American polity, divergence
  from English, 82
American Revolution, 132,
  133-4, 137, 150-51, 154, 157,
  165, 174
Anglo-Saxon law, 83
Anti-cigarette laws, 204
Anti-trust laws, 44
Application of law, nature of,
  78
Appeal (in the old law), 90
Appellate courts, pressure of
  business in, 210
Arrest, 108
Assize, commissions of, 89
Assizes, 98
Attorney General, 107, 150, 182
Attorneys, 156
Austin, John, 10

Bail, 186
Ballantine, Serjeant, 73, 74
Bar, admission to and training
  for, 45, 157-8, 194-5
  as a check on courts, 46, 196
  associations, 156, 193, 196, 207
  circuit, 158, 196
  deprofessionalizing of, 49
  discipline of, 158-9, 195-6
  local, 157-8
  organization of, 155-9, 193-7
Baranelli, case of, 176
"Bargain days," 184
Barristers, 155-6
Beck, Adolf, case of, 71, 72,
  73, 74
Belief and opinion, organized
  meddling with, 203
Benefit of clergy, 102, 111
Bentham, Jeremy, 209
Bills of attainder, 96, 133

217